The Simplicity of Self-Healing

Lisa Warner

Dedication

This book is dedicated to my friends and loved ones who have either lost their struggles with their bodies, or are currently in the midst of struggle.

It is also dedicated to *You*, dear reader! Yes, *You*...the one who is now ready to remember Who You Really Are...the one who is now ready to let go of the struggle with your body and allow yourself to remember your innate well-Being. The one who is now ready to take personal responsibility for your life experience. This book was written *especially* for You. You were with me every step of the way. Your energy is contained within these pages. The words contained within are also *Your* words. This book is Your message to You, I simply agreed to be the one who typed it into my computer. May this book serve to open the door, re-connecting You to the wisdom and Well-Being of Your Soul.

Many Blessings for a healthy, happy and prosperous journey!

Contents

Preface

No problem can be solved from the same level of consciousness that created it. —Albert Einstein

Humanity has been suffering for millennia. Suffering from disease. Suffering from poverty. Suffering from all of the other ills that plague humanity. Isn't is about time that we say, "Enough already!"? Isn't it time that we begin to put an end to all this suffering?

For eons of time, the collective consciousness of humanity has been existing within the confines of the Third Dimension. However, as of December 2012, the doors to the Fifth Dimension and beyond were opened. Huge, expanded realms of consciousness are now available to us, that allow us to create completely new circumstances for ourselves; circumstances of our own choosing.

How do I know this? I am one of the ones who helped to open those doors. Because I have opened those doors and stepped through, I know what lies on the other side. I live on the other side of that doorway.

As our dear Dr. Einstein so wisely stated, we must use a completely different level of consciousness to solve the problems that have been plaguing us. This book is a delivery vehicle for that new consciousness.

Because the concepts and awarenesses contained in this book are very new to the planet, they will often seem to be in direct contradiction to our 'conventional wisdom.' That 'conventional wisdom,' however, has not been able to alleviate our suffering.

Are we now willing to take a *totally different* approach? Is it 'worth the risk' of traveling outside our comfort zone...that comfort zone of pain, fear, disease, stress, lack and limitation into new, 'uncharted' territory? Or is it safer to stay inside our box, where, at least we know what it is like, even if we don't particularly *like* it?

What if a completely different 'comfort zone' is available to us? A new 'comfort zone' of health, vitality, ease, abundance, freedom and joy? A comfort zone where disharmony, disease, lack and limitation *don't even exist*?

What if this is available to you right here, right now? Is it worth the 'risk' to find out?

Would you be willing to let go of your old, comfortable beliefs that are keeping you locked into *dis*-comfort, in lieu of a brand new set of expansive, expanded awarenesses that can lead you into a whole new paradigm of health and happiness?

What if you already know all of this? What if you've simply momentarily forgotten that you knew this...like a bout of amnesia?

This book is designed to help you remember. It is designed to trigger your inner knowing...the part underneath the amnesia. It is not meant to teach you anything. Why? Because it can't teach you something that you already know!

Are you willing to turn your knowing back on? Are you willing to become aware of the vast, inner wisdom you already possess? Are you willing to find out that underneath that amnesia, you are a Being of Grand Magnitude?

Are you willing to remember Your Truth? The Truth of who You Are? I cannot tell you Who You Are...only You can do that!

I'm just here to trigger your memory...

Acknowledgments

I would like to take this opportunity to thank my Mastering Alchemy playgroup partners **Kathy Bradley, Rosemary Marchetta** and **MariaPaz Cuevas** for their unconditional love, support and encouragement. Their contributions to this book and to my life are appreciated beyond words. Without them, this book might never have been birthed. And thank you to **Jim Self,** founder of Mastering Alchemy for everything you've helped me remember, and especially for grouping the four of us together! Thank you *Kathy* and *Rosemary* for contributing deeply insightful chapters to the book which add meaningful content and an extra dimension of love and support for the readers. Thank you *MariaPaz* for your your clear insights and assistance in editing the content, which greatly enhanced the book's clarity and flow.

To **Richard Streuly** for your time and your editor's insights. Your suggestions and positive feedback were extremely helpful, highly encouraging and very much appreciated!

To my dear friend **Joyce Wente**, who encouraged me and cheered me on every step of the way and provided a key piece of the puzzle exactly when I needed it.

I also wish to offer a huge *Thank You* to my dear friend **Stephen Adams** who so graciously and skillfully designed this book and coordinated its publication. Without his wisdom, skill and support, you would not be reading this today.

Without these beautiful Beings, I would not have had the wherewithal to create this book. I am truly grateful to have such kind, loving, generous, talented and supportive human angels in my life.

Introduction

This book is born from experience, inspiration and discovery. It is designed as a guide for Self-Healing, but more than that, it is designed as an energetic space specifically created with the intention of helping You to remember the health, well-being and balance that *You Are* by nature. It is designed to help You align YourSelf with the wellspring of health and vitality that is inherent within you.

Have you temporarily forgotten that health, wealth and well-being are your *natural* state of Being? Is it time to remember? Are you willing to allow yourself to remember who You *really* Are?

Would you be willing to allow all disease to dissolve from your reality? Would you allow radiant health to be your natural state of existence? What would your life be like if disease didn't exist in your world?

I am able to ask these questions because I have already experienced this for myself and I can attest that I literally allowed disease to dissolve from my life. Disease no longer exists in my world. This is my reality. Yes, I see others in *dis*-ease around me and I am aware of how very real their experience is, as I have been there, too. However, I also now realize that a *different* choice is available. That is why I have written this book: to share my experience and insights and show others that there is a completely different reality that is available to be experienced by any and all who are ready and willing to have it.

This book contains the first-hand knowledge I've gained from my personal experience in changing my reality with regard to disease, as well as the wisdom I've gained from the teachings and insights of other 'human angels' who have also 'walked the path' to new levels of awareness and reality.

This book is designed to help you see physical conditions and diseases in a different light. The aim is to provide a clear, easy-to-see-and-understand outline of how physical dis-ease is created on an energetic level, and the simple steps to un-create it and allow the potential for it to dissolve from your reality. (Please don't mistake *simple* for *easy*, although it certainly *can* be...that is for *you* to decide!) It is designed as a tool to facilitate self-empowerment and personal discernment. It is designed to help you tune into *your own* inner strength, intuition, and your *innate ability* to bring your body, mind and spirit into harmony to create vibrant, radiant health...and anything else you desire to create.

But, beware! This book is also designed to poke and prod you, and to provoke you out of the complacency of your old belief systems!

Are You ready to be poked and provoked into new levels of awareness? Are you sure?

Self-Healing through self-awareness is not for the faint of heart! It takes a willingness to be brutally honest with yourself. It takes a willingness to let go of your beliefs...*all of them!* It takes a willingness to replace your *beliefs* with your *knowing*. It takes a willingness to be vulnerable and gentle with yourself. It takes a willingness to love yourself...warts and all. Are you willing to love...You?

This is *not* a 'how-to' book and it will not *tell you what to do.* **It is not meant to be taken as medical advice or to take the place of your doctor's advice.**

This book is offered as a guideline through the realms of consciousness for those who are ready to take full responsibility for the *conscious creation* of their own health and healing. It contains my direct knowing and personal awareness. The insights provided are not merely *theory...they are my direct experience...*they are *my reality.* They are the wisdom gained from my personal journey from health, to disease and back again. *I'm not asking that you believe that what I say is true...No!* I'm asking you to **find Your Truth...Your Inner Knowing.**

The book is designed to 'take the mask off' physical imbalance, illness and disease. Remember when Dorothy in the Wizard of Oz found out that the 'great and powerful Wizard of Oz' was really just a man with a microphone behind a big curtain? He didn't seem so 'great and powerful' after that, did he? Are you willing to find out that your physical dis-ease is not what you think it is?

I'm prepared to show you that your physical imbalance, like the Wizard, is *not* what you think it is (*or* it is *exactly* what you think it is...*you* get to choose!). Whatever your condition is, this book will help you to see it in a new and different light, and, if you're willing, will take you to see who 'the great and powerful Oz' of your physical imbalance really is.

This book also contains tips and suggestions on ways to connect to your own inner wisdom...the innate wisdom of your body and your Soul...the wisdom of *You* that already *knows* how to be radiantly healthy. Do you remember what Dorothy and her friends learned from the Wizard? Do you remember that they each discovered that they already possessed whatever it was that they had been searching for? What if the same is true for you? What if you already possess everything you need to bring yourself back into radiant health? Once we 'remove the curtain' and see physical imbalance and disease for what they really are, and you realize that you already possess the keys to radiant health, it then becomes a relatively simple matter of *becoming aware* and allowing your body to bring itself back into health and balance.

This book also offers ways to connect to the love and support of the angelic realms. The angels are ready, willing and able to lend you assistance any time you are willing to ask for it. The book is about *Self* healing, but that does not mean you have to do it all by yourself. There are angels all around you...including human angels...who are just waiting to be called upon to lend their love, guidance, expertise and support.

This book can give you a much broader perspective from which to view your present circumstance.

Perhaps you may feel some discomfort as some of your patterns and issues get uncovered, and that's a good thing, as long as you can recognize it and embrace it as an opportunity for change. You'll need to be willing to take a look at your 'darkness' in order to change it. And you'll be very surprised to discover that the 'darkness' isn't at all what you thought it was!

You'll need to be willing to let go of many of your old points of view, as those are part of what's creating your condition. This book is designed to help make the process as easy, quick and fun as possible!

You *can* heal yourself! You can heal yourself *by* yourself, or you can enlist the help of a doctor, alternative healer or energy practitioner. You can choose to take medicines, homeopathic remedies, switch to a raw food diet...or none of these! There is no *one right way* to heal yourself. No matter what path you choose, no matter how you choose to do it, no matter who you choose to assist you, *YOU are the one who is responsible for the healing!* If you follow *YOUR OWN* inner guidance, the process will be perfect for you.

Is it a guarantee? Yes!...and *No!* It *is* a guarantee that you can create anything you choose, including a radiantly healthy body. But will you?...*That,* my friend, is for YOU to decide!

Is this Book for You?

Are you ready to reclaim your full power? This book is about personal empowerment: empowering YOU to remember the powerful Being You Are. Are you ready to stop ignoring your inner knowing? Are you ready to stop being a victim? Are you ready to claim your own innate strength, wisdom and ability to create the body (and life) *You* choose? Are you willing to stop looking at *what is* and allow yourself to realize that an even broader, more expanded, *limitless* reality is also available for you to choose? **Are you willing to experience this reality *and yourself* in a completely different way?**

Radiant health is a *choice.* Are you ready and willing to choose it?

This book is for you if:
- You are ready to look at reality from a completely different perspective
- You are willing to stop believing that the 'rules' of this reality are *real* and *unchangeable*
- You are willing to challenge, expand and upgrade your conscious awareness
- You are ready to **have your belief systems challenged**
- You are willing to take *full responsibility* for your creations
- You are ready to learn to trust yourself

- You are ready to *LIVE* the *life you choose* to create
- You are ready to do whatever it takes to start listening to and trusting your own *inner knowing*
- You are ready to learn what is true *for you* and stop accepting other people's truths as your own
- You are willing to let go of all of your beliefs and points of view about what illness is
- You are willing to let go of everything that is no longer working for you
- You are willing to remember the God within...the God You Are
- You are willing to LOVE and TRUST YOURSELF

If you are ready and willing, then **this book is for you!**

This book is based upon *personal truth*...meaning: what has proven to be true based on actual personal experience. It is *your* job to decide what is truth for *You*. What is true for one person (or an entire planet full of people, for that matter!) does not mean it is necessarily true for *You*. You are a *unique* Being! You are a totally unique expression of the All-That-Is. There is NO ONE in all of creation who is just like you. You have your own unique gifts, talents, perspectives and knowingness. It is *crucial* that you learn to discern for yourself what is YOUR truth. We will address this issue throughout the book, as it is a key component in creating wellness.

Are you willing to be discerning?

Are you willing to discover *your own* truths?

If so, then **this book is for you!**

As you read, you are urged to take what resonates as truth for you and leave the rest as just an interesting point of view. You will be encouraged throughout the book to tap into *your own* knowingness. Just because something is true for *Me*, does not automatically mean that it is true for *You*. Because it is true for Me means that it is a *viable, available truth,* but whether you choose to avail yourself of that Truth is *Your choice* and Yours alone. If you feel inclined to argue or disagree with something, become aware of that resistance...it is a key to setting yourself free *if you are willing to use it!*

This book, by design, does not adhere to the traditional uses of capitalization and punctuation. It is not intended to be a literary masterpiece, but rather it is written in such a way to make it a fun,

easy read and to impart specific energies and awarenesses. The use of ..., 'quotes', CAPITALS, *italics,* and **bold** are intentionally used to impart energetic frequencies. If you are offended by 'improper' punctuation, this is a wonderful opportunity to release some resistance and judgement that have accumulated in your system, as resistance and judgement both serve to keep you locked into limitations which eventually become reflected in your body!

This book is designed to present a radically simplified perspective on how we create reality. Upon first glance, it may appear as if the information contained in this book is over-simplified and therefore couldn't possibly be true because, after all, the Universe is a multi-layered, multi-faceted place of vast diversity and complexity. This is true. Our rational minds like to tell us that we need to know *how* everything works. However, do you really have to know all the intricacies of alternators, carburetors, drive trains, transmissions, fuel injection, rods and pistons, etc., in order to drive your car...or can you simply hop in your car and drive? Does your *ability to drive* depend on upon knowing the inner workings of the engine? Of course not.

Do you really want to dismiss something because it seems too simple? What if *simple* is the key to unlocking you from your limitations?

Do you really need to know *how* the universe works in order to change your reality? No! The 'how' is not your job...that job belongs to the universe! Your 'job' is to *create* and then *allow* the universe to support your creation.

Are you willing to give 'simplicity' a try?

If so, then **this book is for you!**

With all that said, *if this book is for you,* then let's dive in and start to explore what is really going on with physical imbalance and how we can begin to change it.

SECTION ONE:

Who are We?

First Things First

Before we get started on our journey from physical imbalance to radiant health, there are a few basic concepts that must be addressed:

The Soul

Every disease, every *dis*-ease, is caused from an imbalance; a dis-harmony; a separation from the truth of our innate well Being. As humans, we operate mainly from our minds and our bodies, while our souls (the infinite, unlimited, non-physical parts of our Selves) are largely forgotten. Body, mind and soul were not meant to be separated; they were meant to work together as one harmonious whole.

Because we've been operating from the separation of these three components, disharmony is rampant. When we bring the soul back into the equation, we bring the knowledge and wisdom of the universe with it. When we reunite Body, Mind and Soul, we become greater that the sum of our parts. When we harmonize Body, Mind and Soul, harmony returns to all areas of our lives, including our cellular structure.

This book is designed to help inspire you to dissolve the rift between You and Your Soul...Your Inner Being...so that you can re-balance your body, re-harmonize your life and re-member Who You Truly Are. When you begin to live from the wisdom of your

Soul, rather than from the limitations of your cognitive mind, you begin to flow with the Universe. When you flow with the Universe, you begin to dance a beautiful dance, fully supported, with the Universe as your partner. When body, mind and soul are no longer separated, they merge into a Oneness that is in full resonance with the Oneness and well-being of the Universe. When You are in full harmony, imbalance cannot exist.

Would you be willing to invite your Soul to come back into your life?

Are you willing to bring yourself into FULL harmony and balance...body, mind and soul? Are you willing to BE your Soul? Are you willing to re-member your Whole Self? Are you willing to see the illusions of this physical reality for what they are and let them go? Do you dare to become the *unlimited* Being You *truly* Are?

Reality

Is *reality* as REAL as you think it is? Is your version of reality *the* reality?

Let's look at this. Is your reality the same as the President of the United States' reality? Meaning: do you think that you and the President see life from the same perspective...do you share the same version of reality? How about the Dalai Lama? Is his reality the same as yours? How about the Pope's reality? How about a homeless person's reality? How about the little child that lives down the block? Are all of these people experiencing the same reality? Can you see that everyone is experiencing their own version of reality? Can you see that there is not just ONE *reality,* but rather many different versions of reality*? What if you could CHOOSE your reality?*

Is there something in your reality that you would like to change? Your body, perhaps?

Are you experiencing an imbalance in one or more areas of your life? What if you could bring that area back into full balance and experience total freedom in that area? What if you could experience a completely different reality in which you were experiencing total harmony, completely free from illness or disease?

Has your body become your prison? Do you feel trapped inside your own body? Do you feel powerless to change your condition? I know exactly what that feels like! I've been there, too!

I'm here to tell you that outside the prison of your current reality, is a completely different reality...a reality of health and vitality. This book is a doorway to that different reality. Outside the dark prison cell is a beautiful reality filled with grass, trees, birds singing, blue skies and sunshine. Would you like to step outside into the light?

The funny thing about your prison cell is that right in the middle of the big, solid cement wall you've been staring at is a doorway you've never noticed. Here...let me open it for you. It was never even locked! You've been free to leave this entire time! And here's the *really* crazy thing: you're already outside in the sunshine! *Yes!*...the greater part of you, the non-physical part of you, is already standing in the sunshine...totally free! Your Soul is standing in the sun, calling to you...*are you ready to come out and play?*

How do I know this? Because I've already experienced it for myself. I'm standing out in the sunshine. I can show you the doorway and hold the door open for you, but you'll have to choose whether or not to step through.

The Divine

You are inextricably connected to the All That Is. The *All That Is* is exactly that: *ALL* that *IS;* everything that exists...everywhere...in all dimensions...seen and unseen...on the Earth, in the Universe and beyond. There is nothing that is excluded from The All That Is. Some call the All That Is: Source, or God, The Creator, Consciousness or The Universe. The All That Is is infinite and cannot be defined by a name. The ancient Hebrews referred to Source, or God as: the One whose name cannot be spoken. It's not because the name is so Holy that it is not allowed to be spoken; it is because *infinite* cannot be defined through words. It includes everything: all things physical, all things non-physical, the solar system, the Earth, love, joy, rocks, trees, angels, energies, anger, fear, stars, flowers, fish, water, thoughts, ideas, air, cats, dogs, slugs and snails. Everything is part of the All That Is, everything is part of Source...including

YOU! You are a piece of The All That Is...a unique piece of God! You and God are made of the exact same substance! You are an individualized, unique expression of the Creator! You are One with God! You cannot be excluded or separated from All That Is; it is impossible. You cannot be 'not God,' because You and God are interconnected within the Oneness of All That Is.

You are One with Source. This is who You Are. You cannot be less. You cannot be more. You cannot be separate. You cannot be excluded. You are a unique expression of God experiencing Itself in human form. You are not broken. The *All That Is* cannot be broken. It is impossible. You are not *wrong* or *less than*, because Source cannot be wrong or less than...Source just *Is*. You are made of Source energy. You *are* Divine Perfection.

You are an Infinite Being here on Earth playing a game of limitation. You are exploring the nature of your Being through the lens of separation and duality. Through the lens of separation, you feel singular. Through *separation* you can feel lost, alone, small, insecure or even superior. *Duality* divides all experiences into opposites: good and bad, love and hate, right and wrong, etc. The crazy thing is, theses are all very real *illusions*. (We'll dive deeper into this as we go along.)

In a simple analogy, You are to Source as a water molecule is to the ocean. The ocean is comprised of bazillions of individual water molecules, all creating one Ocean, while Source is comprised of bazillions of angelic entities, each one a unique, individualized aspect of Source energy.

In the Ocean, some water molecules will sink to the bottom of the ocean where it is cold and dark, others will float to the surface where it is warm and bright, while still others will move to the shoreline where they will be smashed upon the rocks. Each expression of the ocean is beautiful unto itself. Isn't it amazing to watch the beauty and power of the ocean as the waves smash into the rocks and spray high into the air creating rainbows?

A water molecule that is floating on the surface in the warm sun is not having a *better experience* than a water molecule that is being smashed upon the rocks. Each scenario is simply a different aspect of *being the ocean*. In the grand flow of nature, the water molecules at the bottom of the ocean will eventually experience floating on the warm surface.

Just as the ocean is comprised of bazillions of water molecules in different states of *being the ocean,* we are each individual aspects of Source experiencing ourselves in the state of *being human.* A human having the experience of 'floating in the warm sun' is not having a *better experience* than the one who is experiencing being 'smashed upon the rocks.'

Are you willing to stop judging and resisting your life, your body, and your Self, and allow your experience of 'being smashed upon the rocks' to turn into the beautiful rainbow that You Are?

Why Are We Here?

As unlimited beings, fully interconnected in the Oneness of All That Is, there is nothing we are not. We are infinite and unlimited. *Everything* is ours to play with and explore! By using the illusions of *limitation* and *separation* within a realm of physical reality to explore ourselves and our creations, we gain a better understanding of the true nature of our own Divinity. Think of it this way: does one have more appreciation of their health after they have been ill? Can you see how we can gain a better understanding of our true nature by exploring ourselves from a completely different perspective...from the 'opposite' of who we truly are?

By exploring all aspects of limitation while believing that we are separate from the All That Is, we gain a much broader awareness and appreciation of the true nature of what it means to *BE.*

The only way that we can successfully explore this land of limitation is by fully 'forgetting' who we really are. We must don a *veil of forgetfulness* when we enter the physical realm of the Third Dimension. We have to fully *believe* that we are limited and separate in order to be able to fully immerse ourselves in the experience. We have to be fully engulfed in the belly of limitation in order to experience it in all its glory.

Because we *are* unlimited and infinite, we have no fear of entering into our experience of 'forgetting,' because we are fully aware that it is only an experience. We know that no matter what the human story, it is only an experience...and that experience, whatever it is, only adds to and enhances our overall Being-ness. We know that We, the Infinite Being, cannot 'die' or be 'harmed' in any way, therefore, there is nothing to fear about having a human experience. It is just like an actor taking on a difficult role in a film or a play. The actor has no fear of diving deep into the pain, anger, fear or sadness of their character, because they know that it is just a role they are exploring.

We, as Infinite Beings are not afraid to explore the 'hard stuff' either! In fact, the 'hard stuff' is a priority! As Infinite Beings, we do not experience pain, anger, fear, hurt, doubt or separation because those things do not exist within the more expanded realms of the All That Is. Where we come from, everything is in balance and harmony within the Oneness.

So here we are, appearing to be 'lost' and 'separate' in the 'Land of Limitation.' Are we ready to lift our 'veils of forgetfulness' and begin to remember our true nature? That option is now on the table. In fact, the clarion call has gone out from the angelic realms: "Game over! Come on home! You've done a fabulous job in exploring every nook and cranny of lack and limitation! Bravo! Well done! Now lift your veils and come home...We miss You!"

It is now time for us to remember. Many humans have already begun the process of awakening. Are *You* ready?

Beyond the 'Veil'

Science shows us that the universe is holographic. In very simplified terms, continuing with our ocean analogy, if you take the entire ocean and break it down into individual water molecules, EACH individual molecule contains the blueprint of the *entire ocean*. The scientific principle of the holographic universe basically states that everything that *is*...including every cell of your body... contains the blueprint of the **entire** universe.

The physical setting for our human experience is similar to a gigantic holodeck, like we've seen on Star Trek. On the *Starship Enterprise*, the holodeck is a big, empty room into which the computer can project a holographic representation of anything the user desires: a scene from 19th Century London, the ski slopes of Aspen or a whitewater kayak course. The projection appears as if it is 'real' and 'solid' so the user can have their desired experience, whether that be skiing down the slopes or solving a Sherlock Holmes-type mystery. The user defines the parameters of the 'reality' in which they desire to experience themselves, and the computer creates a 'simulated reality' holographic projection to match. Our 'reality' is actually very similar to that! The holographic projection of our 'reality' is designed to directly reflect back to us everything that we believe, like a huge mirror: we create, and the hologram responds by reflecting our creation back to us.

Hint: Remember: we are here exploring ourselves as the *opposite* of who we really are, so therefore, reality appears to be the *opposite* of what it actually is. It appears to us as if 'reality' (the holo-program) already exists and that we are simply reacting to it...while, in fact...we are the programmers...our holodeck experience is the direct result of our programming input (our conscious and *un*conscious thoughts and beliefs).

We believe that reality (the hologram) is real, fixed and solid. We believe that the hologram was here first and that we are subject to its rules. We believe that we are limited and are at the mercy of the hologram. What we don't realize, however, is that *we create* how the hologram appears for us. We also believe that there is only one hologram that all of humanity shares. However, we fail to understand that within that giant, shared hologram, we are each creating our own individual holographic experiences, thereby influencing the giant shared hologram. (A water molecule at the bottom of the ocean might describe the ocean as cold and dark, while a molecule on the surface might describe the ocean as warm and bright...each is having a different experience within *the ocean*.) **Each individual influences the whole.** That means that YOU *are influencing the world*...right here, right now!

We humans have a saying: *I'll believe it when I see it,* indicating that the only way we can experience something is if we can see that it has already been created in the hologram. We don't realize that *we must create it first,* then we will experience it in the hologram. So the *true* statement is actually the direct opposite: *I'll see it when I believe it.*

This means that if you currently have an *unwanted physical condition,* then somewhere along the line you adopted a belief system that dictates that you're prone to physical malady. Because you believed that you were susceptible to the experience, the experience eventually manifested in your reality. You believed in it first, then it showed up in your reality. Now, to experience yourself as healthy, you'll need to let go of your belief in the 'condition' and replace that old belief with the *knowing* of the natural health and wellness of the Infinite Being You Are. As soon as you *know* that you are healthy, then health will be made manifest for you.

Does that sound scary, difficult or complicated? Perhaps it sounds a bit crazy? Don't worry...I'll walk you through all the different aspects of how this works and show you how you can do this for yourself. If you're willing to stick with me, I'll be right there with you every step of the way! This is where we're heading!

The Missing Instruction Manual

Perhaps you've noticed that we're not given a rulebook or instruction manual at birth telling us that we are creating our own realities and outlining the parameters for us. Knowing the parameters from the outset would defeat the purpose. Remember: the point of this experience is to explore ourselves as the *opposite* of who we are, to explore the nature of ourselves as perceived through the lens of limitation and separation, and then find our way *home* to OurSelves by remembering our true, infinite nature. We have to do this through pure trial and error, with much of the emphasis usually placed on the perceived *error* side of the equation. Welcome to physical reality in the Third Dimension!

We awoke one day to find ourselves with tiny little human baby bodies within this physical reality. The world of *form* around us was already filled with wondrous and amazing things! There was so much to explore and discover! It didn't take very long, however, until we began to experience the limitations of third dimensional consciousness.

The Third Dimension is a state of consciousness that is structured. That means that it has specific parameters and rules by which it operates. It is based upon a set of *illusional belief systems* that enable us to experience ourselves as the opposite of who we are.

These illusional belief systems include concepts such as:

Separation: we come from Oneness. We cannot be separated. Ever. However, the *illusion* of separation enables us to explore emotions such as rejection, isolation and the feelings of being *less than* or *superior.*

Duality: 'dual' means two. The illusion of duality enables us to explore 'opposites' such as good and bad, right and wrong, positive and negative. It enables us to explore judgement and criticism. It allows us to believe that 'there are two sides to every coin' and 'you have to take the bad with the good.' It encourages us to embrace the 'positive' experiences and *resist* the 'negative' ones.

Linearity: we believe that we exist along a linear timeline. We believe that we are born, we age then we die. We believe in 'cause and effect' and that there must always be a logical progression for each experience. This illusion clouds our memory of our natural abilities for magic, miracles and instant manifestation. It also allows for the experience of *time.*

Limitation: we believe that we can be, do or have *either* this *or* that. It allows us to define ourselves by having to choose how we represent ourselves within physicality. We believe that our choices are limited, as defined by the hologram and the accumulation of our past experiences. In our natural state, as Infinite Beings, we are truly *un*limited.

Duality keeps 'opposite' experiences paired together. Each pair of 'opposites' mark either end of a spectrum, a 'measuring stick' of sorts...with 'good' on one end and 'bad' on the other, or 'rich' on one side and 'poor' on the other. When we compile all of the available pairs of opposites, they form a 'structure' of sorts that surrounds us. From inside this 'box', our available choices are limited because we don't have access to the choices that are outside of the box.

Outside the 'box' of the Third Dimension, all *limitation* ceases to exist. All of the 'negative' sides of duality, i.e., *hate, illness, lack, isolation, depression,* etc. only exist within the confines of the Third Dimension. Outside of the Third Dimension, concepts such as *safety* cease to exist, because there is nothing that is *unsafe.* Outside the Third Dimension, a concept such as *ease* takes on a much deeper, richer, more expansive meaning which includes *flow, harmony, fulfillment, peace and joy.* And outside the Third Dimension, *Love* ceases to be just an emotion, but turns into the power that moves the tides, changes the seasons and keeps the planets in their orbits...it is the *fabric* of the entire universe.

For most of our human history, we have been stumbling around inside the *box* of the Third Dimension without knowing exactly how it operates. We are Creator Beings. We create. Constantly. We are constantly, continually creating our realities in every moment. We simply have not been realizing it. If you had realized it, you would have created it a bit differently, no? Well, here's your chance!

It wasn't until very recently in our history (the end of the Twentieth Century) that larger groups within humanity began to *awaken*, 'put the pieces of the puzzle' together and began to start understanding the natural laws of the universe which govern how this reality is created. Up until this point in history, that knowledge was held by only a very select few mystics, shamans, sequestered yogis, avatars and masters like Jeshua (Jesus) and Buddha. Fortunately for us, this knowledge is becoming readily available for anyone who is ready to embrace it. The self-help and personal growth industries are booming! Major breakthroughs in quantum physics are showing us the mechanics of quantum energy. Humanity is now rapidly gaining access to the information about who we really are, why we're here and how the universe works. Many of us are now *removing our veils*.

Once we begin to understand what the Third Dimension actually is and how it operates, then we can begin to understand how we created our present circumstances and how we can change them. It is time to throw out the old 'rules' that were keeping us locked into dis-ease and limitation and step up into the realms of awareness that allow us to *consciously create* the lives of our dreams!

As we awaken and begin to see through the illusions of limitation that are held within the Third Dimension, we are able to remove our 'veils of forgetfulness' and step out of the rigid consciousness of the Third Dimension and step into the *unlimited* realms of the Fifth Dimension and beyond. This is referred to as *The Shift, Enlightenment, Awakening* or *Ascension*. I'm only mentioning this here, as these are terms that you're going to start hearing much more often within mass consciousness.

The Shift refers to the fact that we are now beginning the process of *shifting* out of the Third Dimension and into the higher, or more expanded realms of conscious awareness. In order for us to accomplish this, we must be willing to remember who we truly are. We must see the illusions of duality and separation for what they are...*illusions*...then *let them go* and reclaim our powers as the grand, infinite Creator Beings we Are.

Who We Really Are

Let's take a moment to examine a very simplistic explanation of who we think we are from within the third dimension.

Most likely, you were taught that you have a soul. And it is also quite likely that you learned that this soul is a non-physical part of you that is off somewhere else and you may be reunited with it after you die. This is part of the *illusion of separation* in this reality. In actuality, you cannot be separated from your Soul; *it is impossible;* You *are* your Soul...you have simply shut off your awareness to the vast, non-physical, infinite part of You, in order to pretend that you are a limited human. *The good news* is that you can turn that awareness back on!

In fact, **it is absolutely essential that you re-open your awareness!** Here's why: your current circumstance of illness or imbalance has been created from *unawareness*. Would you have created your current physical imbalance on purpose? Of course not! You were *unaware* that you were creating it, so in order to *un*create it, **you must become aware of what you are creating.** We'll dive more extensively into this as we go along.

Although these are very simplistic explanations of the nature of reality, they are purposely designed as such. Reality really *is* just that simple, yet it is also vastly more complex. In this reality, complexity is designed to keep the cognitive mind in a state of *searching* for answers and *figuring it out,* which ultimately keeps us from our greater awareness...our *inner knowing. Searching* and *figuring out* are designed to keep us locked into the illusion of limitation by causing us to look *outside* of ourselves for answers that are contained *within* us. Does the All That Is need to go searching for answers or try to figure stuff out? No! Why? Because all the answers are already contained within! When the All That Is asks a question, it remains perfectly still and simply...*becomes aware*...of the answer! *What if we can do the same?* Remember the holographic universe: the entire universe is already contained within every cell of your body...therefore, all answers already exist within you.

Complexity (searching and trying to figure it out) keeps us *locked in the maze* of this reality. Would you be willing step outside of the maze? Would you be willing to allow life to be *simple* for a change? After all, has *figuring out* the complexities of life ever actually worked for you? What if life cannot be *figured out?* What if making it *simple* was actually the key you've been searching for? Would you be willing to consider that possibility?

Your Body

Since you are not separate from your soul, then *who you appear to be* (physical human) is **not** who you *really are*; it is an **experience you are having**. The *illusion of separation* causes us to believe in the division of body, mind and soul (or spirit). We come to believe that these are three individuated components of who we are and that they function separately. This is not the case.

When body, mind and soul are perceived as separate, disharmony *has to* occur. It has to occur because in truth you are One...not 'three pieces' of One. In order to bring ourselves back into harmony (vibrational alignment), we must bring body, mind and soul back into harmonic resonance... into Oneness. Ideally, we then function as our *soul.* Our *body* then serves as the vehicle through which we experience physical reality and our *mind* becomes the interface mechanism between the non-physical and physical realms, interpreting the desires of the Soul from the non-physical realms into the physical realm and transmitting the physical experiences back to the Soul in the non-physical.

While playing in the game of Limitation, we forget that it is an illusion. We believe that we are our bodies. However, you are not your body, nor are you your circumstances. You *have* a body and you are *experiencing* your circumstances, but they are not who you *are.* This is another essential piece of the puzzle that you must allow yourself to *become aware* of in order to consciously re-create your reality and successfully change the state of your health. Reminder: You *Are* an infinite, unlimited Being who is experiencing itself within the parameters of limitation.

Your *body* is the vehicle through which you get to explore this physical reality. Without your beautiful body, you would not be able to be here on Earth. You would not have had this life, you would not have had any of the amazing experiences you've had in this lifetime. Your body's job is to be the vehicle through which you experience yourself in physicality, and it is designed to be a direct reflection of your thoughts, feelings, beliefs and attitudes about yourself and this reality. The state of health of your body is a direct reflection of your present set of beliefs about yourself and this lifetime. We'll explore more about this as we go along.

Your *mind* is designed to be the interface mechanism...the connector between body and soul. It is designed to act as an interpretive device. However, because we have essentially pushed our soul out of the picture...placed it off in another realm to be picked back up after we die...the mind has been trying to 'fill in' for the wisdom of the soul. The mind was never designed to 'house' the wisdom of the soul...think of it this way...which is bigger: the mind or the soul? You see, the mind is contained inside the soul...the wisdom of soul cannot be contained inside the mind...but that is how we have been trying to operate inside this game of *Limitation*. That's another example of how things in this reality are actually the opposite of what is really True.

When *body, mind and soul* are functioning harmoniously as One, the *mind* is quieted, for it no longer needs to go searching for answers, nor does it need to try to figure things out. The answer lies where the question is asked. The Soul is in harmony (in Oneness) with The All That Is, and all answers are contained therein. Therefore, when a question is posed, the Soul simply *becomes aware* of the answer...no searching or 'figuring out' necessary. This is why we find ourselves 'trapped' in the maze of this reality...we ask a question and then go running off to look for answers, while all the while the answer is found right where the question is asked.

Your body was designed for well-being. It was designed to be a self-rejuvenating vehicle of wellness. When a bone breaks, it automatically mends itself. Bruises, strains and sprains automatically begin rebalancing themselves. Medical science tells us that every cell of the entire body is replaced once every seven years. The body was built to last! It was designed to continually rebalance and regenerate itself. So why doesn't it?

The only reason that the natural rebalance/rejuvenation cycle becomes distorted is because the natural flow of source energy (the energy of well-being and balance that continually flows from Source) gets distorted or blocked by our limiting belief structures.

For instance, the hologram appears to dictate that we get old then die. Because the hologram contains the construct of linear time, we believe that there is always a beginning, a middle and an end, therefore our life stories must reflect that belief back to us. Because we hold *absolute* beliefs (such as, we 'get old' then 'die'), those *absolutes* form belief 'structures' that preclude all other possibilities. We have locked ourselves into our beliefs.

We hold an image of what health and vitality look like when we are teenagers, which greatly differs from the image of what we think health and vitality look like when we're eighty. Because we believe that we have much more health and vitality as teenagers than we do at eighty, our bodies must reflect that belief back to us. Because that belief is agreed upon by all of mass consciousness, we then believe *'that's just the way it is'* and we follow the path to aging by default. This is a direct result of the misperception that the hologram pre-exists and we are merely reacting to *what is*. Remember: this belief is backwards. First we create, then we see it in the hologram.

It's fun to note that I've been seeing the term 'de-aging' being used in the media lately, so the illusion of aging is actually beginning to unravel. I noticed a trailer for a medical talk show on TV that was showing women who were already de-aging, appearing to get younger. As we discover and de-bunk these old illusions, we are able to re-create our realities in *amazing* ways! Would you be willing to allow your body to rejuvenate itself?

We also believe that our bodies are susceptible to illness and disease. After all, we see the *proof* around us every day, don't we? Not only do we see friends and family with illnesses and disease, we are inundated with commercials on television that tell us that we need to take this medication and that pill, and that if you have any of 'these' symptoms then you might have 'this' disease. It is as if we are drowning in disease-infested waters and we can't see the island of health and vitality that is just a few short swim strokes away.

Because we are constantly immersed in these beliefs of sickness and disease, we begin to forget that health and wellness are **normal**. We begin to think that illness is *inevitable* and we being to start planning for theses diseases. We've switched our 'normal' from wellness to disease. We think that, *'my mother had this, so I'm prone to it too'*...or *'everyone at work has it, so I'm probably next'*...or *'I hope I never get cancer.'* These thought patterns and beliefs are what your body will reflect back to you.

Can you begin to see how we create illness and disease? What we are focusing our attention on, whether *consciously* or *unconsciously*, must show up in our reality. Remember: we create first, then the hologram reflects our creations back to us.

By becoming aware of our thoughts and beliefs, we can begin to see *how* we are creating whatever it is that we are creating. If we wish to begin creating different results, we must begin by reassessing our limiting thought patterns and belief systems. We must begin to turn off the 'limitation factor' in our beliefs, and return ourselves to the unlimited Beings we truly are so we can re-open our connection to the infinite well-being of Source.

You Are God

Does that statement grab your attention? Does it sound blasphemous?

Does it offend you?

Did you experience some sort of reaction in your system?

If you are feeling some sort of energy around that statement... great! It means that you are holding beliefs that you are either resisting or defending. The reaction you are feeling is the same resistance that has gotten caught in the cells of your body. It will become very important to begin noticing each time you feel resistance and reaction.

Let's look at this more in depth.

To begin with, let's examine the statement itself: You Are God. This is a key to unlocking you from whatever is not serving you in your life.

The 'programming' of this reality is based in the concept of separation. It teaches us that we are separate from each other, that we are small and insignificant, that we are separate from God and even that we are separate from our own souls. Nothing could be further from the truth. We are Infinite Beings, and as such, we are in *Oneness* with All That Is...or God. As *One* with God, we are made of the exact same substance as God...we are 'duplicates' of God. We cannot be *not God*. You are God. I Am God. As God, how easy is it to re-balance your body? Are you willing to Be the God You Are?

As integral parts of God, we each have all of the resources of the entire Universe at our disposal. We are unlimited Creator Beings and the Universe responds to our every desire. The only thing that can possibly block the flow of well-being from the all-loving, infinitely abundant Universe is *ourselves*.

How do we block the flow? Let's take a look. As you read the following statements, do you feel a 'charge' with any of them?

YOU are God. (Does this still make you feel uncomfortable?)

You are infinitely abundant.

There is absolutely *nothing* wrong with you.

Cancer does not exist.

Well...how did you do? Did you feel an emotion? Did your pulse speed up? Did your mind kick into high gear with critical remarks?

Great!

If you can begin to notice whenever you feel resistance, you will begin to find out where you are working against yourself and blocking the flow of well-being. Resistance feels like pressure. It makes you feel uncomfortable or angry or sad.

Each of us is the Creator of our own life experience.

Did that statement cause a reaction? (This would be a good opportunity to take note.) Perhaps you thought, "*No way!* I did *not* create this!"

Well, yes, you did. And that's the good news! (Are you taking note of your reactions?)

Obviously you didn't create your condition *on purpose*. You created it by turning off your awareness. That's good news, because anything that *you* created, *you* can also un-create!

This is crucial for you to understand.

22

It is crucial that you take responsibility for creating your condition. Why? Because if you created it, you can also re-create it (create it differently). If you insist that you *did not* create it, then you are a victim. Victims are powerless to change their circumstances. You are a Creator...you are NOT a victim.

You Have Choice

The illusion of this reality teaches us that we are exactly the opposite of who we really are. It teaches us that we are small, that we are separate, we are vulnerable and that we are not worthy. Because our natural state is Oneness and harmony, we instinctively begin to try to harmonize ourselves with the people and the hologram around us to try to *fit in* to this reality. We try to return to Oneness while functioning inside a box of separation and limitation. As we come to find out, that doesn't work particularly well! (In order to return to Oneness, we must step *outside* the Third Dimensional 'box' of separation and limitation!)

In our misguided efforts to find oneness within separation, we begin by trying to please others...in an effort to create harmony, and to try to 'fit in' with *who we think they expect us to be.* As children, we're told by parents and teachers what to do and how to act, and we follow their directions, even when we know differently. We start giving up our own truths, thinking that the grown-ups must know *better.* We start to compromise our Selves to please others because we love them and want to make them happy.

How long have you been trying to *fit in* here on Earth?

How long have you been trying to be *right?*

How long have you been trying to *not be wrong?*

How long have you worried about what others might think of you?

How long have you been trying to mold yourself into the perfect friend, partner or parent?

How long have you been living *for* other people?

How long have you been placing your needs *last?*

When was the last time you did something for the sheer joy of it?

When was the last time you truly *received*...without any agenda, without wondering how to *return the favor* or without feeling the need to *pay back* the giver...just the pure act of *unconditional receiving?*

When was the last time you gifted to someone, not to just to make *them* happy, but rather, for the feeling of pleasure that *You would receive* through seeing their pleasure?

How long have you been telling yourself that you're not good enough, not smart enough, not beautiful enough, not thin enough, not rich enough? When are you going to stop being *not enough?*

How often do you place others' needs ahead of your own?

How often do you make work a priority above pleasure?

How often do you make sacrifices for someone else?

You see, these are all ways in which you give up your power to the constructs of this reality. This reality tells us to not be *Self-ish;* to place others first; to ignore the Self; to sacrifice the Self for the greater good. It even teaches us that to place our own needs first is wrong! It also teaches us that it is better to give than to receive... sending the impression that receiving is selfish or wrong.

However, each time we place others either 'before' or 'above' us, we make ourselves *less than;* each time we allow someone else's needs to be more important than our own, we are telling ourselves we're not worthy. We dishonor ourselves when we place ourselves last.

We become trained to be more focused on giving than on receiving. We give to our kids, our spouses, our aging parents, we give to organizations and causes, we give our time and our money...but are we also *receiving* in equal measure? The universe is in a constant state of balance...if you are giving more than you are receiving, you are out of balance. Are you allowing the universe to shower you with its unending flow of miraculous gifts? Did you *receive* the kiss of sunshine on your cheek or the beauty of that flower that was blooming its brightest just for you? When you asked for guidance from the angels, did you *receive* their answers? When we become focused on our energy flowing outward (giving), we shut off our awareness to the energy that is also flowing inward *to* us...we shut off our receiving.

You see, by ignoring the Self, we are out of integrity with the All That Is. We have each come here to *BE our own unique Selves.*

That is our ONLY job! We each have come here with our own unique gifts and talents to *enhance* this reality with our presence. We are each God, the Creator, experiencing itself through our own unique expression. It is our job to *BE* authentically our *Selves*...that is our *GIFT* to this reality! We become trained that we have to *DO* in order to *BE*...that we have to *DO* something in order to *BE*... happy, healthy, wealthy or wise. Can you see the illusion?

If you were BEing The Authentic You, the *pure essence* of the infinite You, You would automatically be in harmony with everyone and everything around you. You would not be trying to fix or change others, yourself or your circumstances. Your circumstances would automatically be in alignment with well-being, because the essence of You *is* Well-Being! You would not be looking to be fixed, nor would you be looking to fix another; God does not need to be fixed. *You* do not need to be *fixed* because *You are NOT broken;* it is impossible.

If you are experiencing any form of lack or limitation in your experience, it is an indication that you have been denying your True Self. You've been trying to fix and change yourSelf in order to 'fit in' to the constructs of this reality. **You were NOT born to fit in... You were born to NOT fit in!** *You came here to be unique!* You are a unique expression of the Creator...that is your *JOB!* And the best part of that is: *You can NOT screw it up; You cannot get it wrong!* That, too, is impossible!

Would yo be willing to see the true gift that you are?

Would you be willing to stop judging yourself?

Would you be willing to allow yourself to *BE* the authentic *You?*

Would you be willing to start *receiving* unconditionally?

Would you be willing to allow yourself to *NOT* fit in?

Would you be willing to stop trying to change your circumstances...and allow them to naturally rebalance as you to return to Your *True Nature?*

Would you be willing to follow *YOUR* joy?

Would you be willing to start putting your Self first?

Would you be willing to trust your Self?

Would you be willing to appreciate your Self?

Would you be willing to LOVE your Self?

...This is how to return to vibrant, radiant health!

There are no tricks. There are no secrets. There are no methods or procedures to follow. There are no healers that must be consulted and no gurus to follow.

There are no experts who hold *your* answers.

YOU *are* the expert! There is no other Being in all of creation that knows you better than...*You!* YOU possess the answers.

YOU hold the key to your own Well-Being. YOU are the Creator.

YOU are the chooser. What do You *choose?*

YOU *cannot* make the 'wrong' choice!

There are no *right* choices and *wrong* choices...there are only *choices. Right* and *wrong* are illusions...they are simply judgements and conclusions based in duality.

Are you willing to choose *YOU?*

Are you willing to stop trying to be who you think other people want you to be?

Are you willing to choose JOY?

Are you willing to *BE* happy?

Are you willing to BE *good enough*...right here, right now...in this very moment?

Are you willing to *accept* and *receive* the greatness of *You?*

Are you willing to BE the center of your own Universe...Be-ing the Love and the Truth of You...spreading your own vibrant, radiant beauty and well-being to everyone around you?

Are you willing to stop pretending that you're broken, that you're not good enough, that you don't deserve...and start being the Light and the Love that You came here to *Be?*

If you are experiencing something that you deem as undesirable, then You have the Divine Right to change it. You have *CHOICE.*

How do You Choose to Experience Yourself?

We've already established that you came to Earth to experience yourself within the realm of Physicality. Let's look at this a little bit closer.

You came to Earth to experience Yourself...within the realm of physicality.

You came to Earth to experience Your Self.

Do you see what this means?

You came to Earth to experience Your *Self*. 'Physicality' is just the backdrop for your experience.

Because we don the 'veil' when we arrive on Earth, that 'veil' has caused us to forget who we are. That 'veil' has caused us to believe that 'who we are' is defined by the physicality (external circumstances) around us. We have been 'defining' ourselves by our external circumstances...I'm poor, I'm not pretty, I'm too tall, I'm better than, I'm faster than, I'm not as smart as, etc. We define ourselves by comparing and contrasting ourselves to others and to our circumstances. We use 'others' as our measuring stick to tell us who we are...and then we believe it!

We use our external circumstances to define who we are on the inside.

Do you realize that no one else can define who *You* are? It is impossible. Nothing outside of you can define who you are on the inside. You Are that You Are...you are whoever you choose to be. Can you see the grand illusion?

You define You. *You* choose how you experience yourself. No one else can choose that for you. No one else can tell you who you are or how you must experience yourself. Not only is it impossible, it's simply not their place. It's YOUR place to decide how *you* wish to experience *yourself.*

Do you wish to experience yourself as healthy? Wealthy? Happy? A winner? A loser? A lover? A fighter? All of these, or none of these? You get to choose! And...you can't make a wrong choice! It's *your* experience...the experience *you* choose. No one else can choose for you...unless you allow them to, by *buying into* their perceptions.

Now...do you see how you have given up your power to external circumstances? Has someone told you that life must be hard? Money is hard to come by? Health is a challenge? You're not smart enough? Your body shape isn't ideal?

If you were alone on the planet...no one else around...how would you choose to experience yourself? Healthy? Fit? Active? Happy? Would you be the same person you are today? Remember: we're talking about the core essence of you...Your Being...who you ARE on the inside. How would you be different if there was no one to interfere with you?

Without other people meddling with your experience, who would you choose to be? What if no one had ever told you that you life was hard? Would you choose *easy?* If no one else existed, would you be beautiful? Would you even have a concept of *ugly?* Would there be any reason to be *not good enough?* Of course not!

How are you currently choosing to experience yourself? Capable? Secure? Uncertain? Unlucky? A winner? A loser? Not good enough? Better than those over there?

Why not try this little exercise:

Pretend that you are the only human on the planet. If you're not psyched about being alone, then pretend that the planet is filled with angels and fairies who are here to play with you and to love and support you in every way, *unconditionally.* As the only human, you have complete freedom. You can go anywhere, do anything and BE whoever you choose. There's no one to tell you that you are bad, or wrong, or not good enough or that you're going to 'inherit' some disease. How would you choose to experience yourself?

Would you choose to be happy? Creative? Playful? Silly? Angry? Frustrated? Would you even know 'angry' or 'frustrated'? Would you be fit and healthy?

If you chose *happy, creative* and *playful,* what do you think your life would look like? Would the angels and fairies join you in creating happy, playful circumstances? Would the world around you reflect your choice to experience yourself as happy, creative and playful? Do you see how this works?

Take some time and write down how you would choose to experience yourself in this utopia. Come up with a list of words. Feel them as you write them. Realize that as you feel those things, they exist within you right now! You can begin to experience those things *NOW* simply by focusing on them.

Our current experience of reality has trained us 'backwards,' causing us to believe that something or someone needs to *be a certain way* in order for us to *feel good,* or *be happy,* or to be *sure of ourselves.* We've been looking at our reflection in the mirror of other people's perceptions, believing that is who we are. But we are not what is outside of us!

We are our core essence. We are who we choose to be. We can choose how we wish to experience ourselves...happy, lucky, healthy, wealthy, winners, losers, outcasts or misfits. Whatever we project ourselves as, gets reflected back to us in our surroundings.

Do you think that if your circumstances are currently causing you *distress* that you cannot *be happy?* Are you sure?

Can you remember a time when you felt *playful?* Go ahead... give it a try! Or just imagine yourself being playful for a moment. Need some ideas? How about sweetly teasing your sweetheart just to see their beautiful smile...or playing in a big pile of fallen leaves... or playing with a puppy or kitten. Imagine *playful...*

Take a few moments to really FEEL *playful!*

Do you notice that you feel more lighthearted? Did a smile sneak across your face? Do you feel a little *happy?*

You see, you just found *playful* and *happy* simply by focusing your attention on them. They are right there inside you...all the time. You've just shifted your focus away from them.

How do you wish to experience yourself? Stressed...happy... outcast...accepted...in love...lonely? All of these are choices. You have free choice. You can choose to experience *anything* you desire! If you think that your circumstances dictate your choices, realize that is backwards. Your choices dictate your circumstances.

Now...I'll ask again: *how do you choose to experience yourself?*

SECTION TWO:
Creating and Re-Creating

It All Begins with a Thought

Where did this disease come from?

Everything that is in physical form originated in the realm of the non-physical before it came into physical being.

What does that mean?

Well, in very simple terms, think of the chair you are sitting on. Before it came into physical reality, the chair was just a *concept*. Then, the concept turned into a *desire* to physically create the chair. It began as an idea, a non-physical thought form. That idea was then fueled by the *emotion* of desire... the desire to see the idea come to physical fruition. Then, in order to get the non-physical idea to appear as the solid chair you are sitting on, focused attention was required and a series of action steps had to be taken.

So, what does a chair have to do with the disease that I experience in my body?

Well, the process of bringing a disease into your body is very similar to the way a chair is brought into being: it all begins with a thought. First there is a thought...a concept of *disease*. Then, in order for disease to be brought into physical form, emotion and focused attention are required.

The formula goes like this: thought + emotion + focused attention = physical manifestation.

So...'disease exists' + 'I'm afraid of disease' + 'What's wrong with me, What's wrong with me, What's wrong with me...' = disease.

31

Once the *concept* of disease is accepted as a potential reality, that potential reality becomes 'activated' by a *negative emotion*. The negative emotion (anger, fear, depression, etc.) sends the body a message: *I'm not okay.*

For any physical disease, the *focused attention* comes in the form of continued **resistance**...which is felt in the body. The resistance comes in one the myriad forms of: *'I'm not okay', 'I'm in danger,' or...'there must be something wrong with me.'* Just like there are millions of different concepts for 'chairs' ranging from packable camping chairs to wooden bar stools, from overstuffed armchairs to sleek leather reclining seats on a private jet...there are just as many variations on the concept *I'm not okay,* hence, the many different types of diseases.

These thoughts of *I'm not okay* begin from very early childhood. For instance, Mommy screams and yells and snatches you away as you reach up to touch the pretty red burner on the stove...*uh oh! I must have done something wrong.* The toddler on the playground bumps into you and pushes you to the ground... *ouch! He's mean to me!* Over the course of your life, the incidents become larger and more *significant.* Your first love rejects you, you get fired from a job, you get divorced...

The more *significance* we place on a 'negative' experience, the more likely we are to hold onto the negative emotional imprint the incident left with us. The negative emotion experienced with the event becomes imprinted, or *locked* into our energetic system, which is held within our cellular structure.

With each subsequent activation of a similar negative emotion, the imprint becomes magnified. What begins as a general *dis-ease,* through focused attention (feeling negative emotions repetitively) eventually turns into *disease.*

The pattern may look something like this: it begins with 'Mommy yelled at me, so I must be bad' and progress to 'I don't fit in, nobody likes me' in high school, to 'he dumped me, I'm not good enough' to 'my marriage ended, I'm worthless' and finally 'I have heart disease.'

All of your beliefs about who you are and what life is, are reflected back to you through your body, because that is its job. Your body, who loves you unconditionally, is designed to show you when you are holding beliefs that do not support your unlimitedness.

32

Your body has been communicating to you, but you just haven't been aware of the message.

The good news is, that once you begin to understand this, it becomes easier to make 'course corrections' in your thought patterns and belief systems by becoming aware of what limiting beliefs of *I'm not okay* you're holding in your system. As you become *aware* of your patterns of thought and limiting beliefs and begin to consciously change the ones that are getting in your way, you'll begin to see changes in your physical reality.

What kinds of beliefs are currently blocking the flow of your well-being?

Is the world a wonderful place?

Do you love life? Is life a chore?

Are you *sick* of living like this?

How much pain do you see in the world around you?

Were you dealt a 'bad hand' in this lifetime?

What are you constantly worrying about?

Do you even *like* yourself?

Would your Soul have a different answer to these questions? Take note! The difference between *your* answers and the answers your Soul would give...are the keys to unlocking you! Your Soul is always in a state of love, harmony and balance. It doesn't experience depression, fear or anxiety. Only the human part of you can experience that. Your Soul...the non-physical aspect of YOU, is infinite and has ALL of the resources of the universe available to it... YOU have infinite choice, but you must be willing to choose. If you can start to realize that you have a 'higher,' more expanded and balanced perspective available to you, you can begin to become aware of a different reality from which to choose.

Begin to look at your thoughts and beliefs about yourself, your life and the world around you. Begin to notice when something makes you feel good and when something triggers you into feeling bad. Begin to notice. Become aware. Only the human part of you that has been wearing the veil of forgetfulness can feel bad...what might your Soul be feeling? What other options are available for you to focus your intention upon?

You must *become aware* of when you're feeling limited, and be willing to make the choice to feel differently in order to begin to change your circumstances. Remember: you've been *unaware* until now, re-acting out of habit...now it's time to wake up, become aware of where you've been limiting yourself and be willing to choose differently.

Remember Your Natural State of Being

The Universe is in a constant state of balance and harmony. The planets revolve in total harmony with the sun. Water is constantly seeking its own level of balance. Nature is in a constant state of renewal.

Throughout the Universe, there is a constant, steady, state of balance and well-being emanating from Source. The universe is abundant! It is filled with potential!

Did you know that there is no such thing as a steady flow of *lack?* or *disease?* or *limitation?* It is *impossible.* Do you know why? Because they're *illusions!*

There is only well-being and abundance within the LOVE that *is* Source, God, the Creator, the Universe, the All That Is. You are an aspect of the Creator. You (your Soul Self) is always in balance and well-being.

Do you have *any idea* how much *effort* it takes to resist the *natural flow of the Universe?* How much effort it takes to *refuse to receive* the gifts of love, ease, balance, abundance and well-being that the Universe is constantly offering? Do you have any idea of the power that you possess that allows you to make the illusion of this reality seem so very *real?*

As an Infinite Being, You (the broader, non-physical You) are in a constant state of harmony and well-being. It is impossible for You, as a Being, to be sick or diseased. It is only you, as a limited human, that can experience dis-harmony and dis-ease. If you are currently experiencing disharmony or disease, it is because you have closed off your awareness to your true, unlimited nature and are blocking the natural flow of well-being by maintaining a contrary perception. When you are able to recognize this, you can then clear the limiting patterns of beliefs or behaviors (misperceptions) that are blocking the flow and re-establish the connection to your Infinite Being. When you (the human) are in harmony with You (the Infinite Being) the symptoms of dis-ease will disappear.

So the questions then become:

Are you willing to remember who you truly are?

Are you *willing to receive* the balance, vitality and well-being that are natural to You?

Are you ready to heal yourself? Are you *willing* to heal yourself? There is no one else who can heal you.

There are no methods, medications, physicians, healers, or witch doctors who have the power to heal you without your active, conscious choice for wellness. You can use certain foods, supplements, methods or medications and you can allow physicians, healers, friends or witch doctors to *assist* you, but the ultimate choice for health is yours and yours alone.

The only one who can heal you is YOU. Period. *You* are the Creator of your reality. No one else can create *for* you...they can only create *with* you. You must take full responsibility for your own creation. You are the Creator: You choose to create something... the universe responds. *Ask and it is given:* that's a Universal Law. What are you asking for? Are you allowing the Universe to gift to you? What are you choosing to create?

Health is natural. Health is normal. Health is who You *are*. Why are you resisting it?

Why are you choosing imbalance, when you could more easily choose balance? Balance is natural. Imbalance takes a lot of effort through resistance. Balance takes *no effort*.

Are you willing to stop resisting life? Are you willing to stop resisting You? Are you willing to receive?

I realize that this all may sound overly simplistic, but it really *IS* that simple. It's just not always *easy*.

How easy (or difficult) it is to bring your life and a your body back into balance is completely up to YOU.

How to Recognize What is Blocking the Flow of Well-Being

Become Aware — Notice What Triggers You

Since you have been operating in '*Un*-aware mode' for quite some time, now would be a good time to press the 'aware' button to turn your awareness back on! It will be through *becoming aware* that you will be able to change your reality.

So how do we become aware?

The first step is to *choose* to become aware. Make a very clear choice that you are now going to become aware. That means to stop reading for a moment, sit quietly, breathe, get clear and focused, and then very clearly state your intention to become aware. Stating your intention out loud and/or writing it down on a piece of paper will help to amplify the power of your choice by bringing it more concretely into the physical realm.

Note: 'lip service' won't do! Just saying, *'yeah...I'll become aware'* will not do you any good! You must make a very clear choice: *"YES! Becoming aware is of ultimate importance to me! I choose to really change my circumstances and I will do that by becoming aware of my negative, limiting habits and patterns! Becoming aware is KEY to my own success! YES! I choose to BE AWARE!"*

The next step is to recognize what *flow* feels like and what *resistance* feels like. It is crucial to be able to notice these feelings *in the moment*. In order to change your reality, you'll have to be able to change the **resistance** into **flow** *on command*. This may sound like a huge task, but once you get the hang of it, it can actually become a fun game to play...how much well-being can I allow to flow through me today?

Flow: feels good. It feels light, it feels expansive, it feels joyful, it feels optimistic, it feels happy. Flow is your TRUTH. Flow is your natural, true state of Being. Flow takes *no effort*. Flow is giving and receiving, accepting and allowing.

Resistance: feels heavy, constrictive, judgmental or sad. *Resistance* is anything that causes you to feel bad. Resistance is heavy; it is sad; it is *not true* for you! You are, by nature, light, free and at ease. So it is very important to be able to recognize when you are feeling resistance and then be able to shift it. Now, of course, there will be times when you will feel sadness, or pain or anger; you're here to experience the fullness of the human condition, after all! However, under normal, healthy circumstances, these emotions will be felt fully and then allowed to release. They do not become trapped in your cellular structure. It is when the emotions are held onto and not allowed to release that they begin to get 'stuck' in the body. They become your 'default' setting. We're intending to change your 'default' from *resistance* to *flow*.

To begin to recognize where you are holding resistance, begin to notice when something or someone 'triggers' you into an emotional reaction. If something triggers you to become very defensive, depressed or emotional, that is where you are holding resistance. Resistance is born from *judgements* and *conclusions*.

A *judgement* is born when you think that something should be different from what it is. It comes from holding strict belief systems of *right* and *wrong, good* and *bad.* In reality, everything is only energy.

Energy is neither good nor bad, right nor wrong: it's just energy. It is our judgements that place our experiences of that energy in those dualistic boxes.

Would you be willing to let go of your judgements? Especially the *self* judgements?

Energy is infinite. Energy, by nature, is free-flowing. It's not meant to be put in 'boxes' of judgement and limitation.

Would you be willing to open all of the boxes where you've stuck your energy and it's now gotten trapped in your cellular structure?

Right and *wrong, good* and *bad* are simply your perceptions. They were the *tools* of the old, 3-D reality and they are no longer required. Your judgements are the filters through which you experience reality. *Are you willing to clear those filters?* **Can you have an experience without putting a label (judgement) of good or bad, right or wrong on it?**

A **conclusion** stems from a decision you've made about something. I'm unlucky, I'm ugly, she hates me, it's unfair...are all examples of conclusions. Are they even true?...*No!* When you come to a conclusion, then the universe must reflect that back to you, whether it is true or not. Once you make a conclusion, you also automatically shut off your awareness to anything that might be contrary to that conclusion. For instance, let's say you go on a date with a great person and come to the conclusion that they are *the one* for you. You will immediately shut off your awareness to the fact that they are actually still dating other people. With each successive date, you fall deeper in love, yet you don't allow yourself to see that they are not on the same wavelength. As you get more intense with the relationship, they actually start to push you away.

Soon they begin to become resentful and start to take advantage of you, while all the while you still are working under the *conclusion* that they are *the one*, because you've shut off your awareness to any other possibility.

*Would you be willing to release all of the conclusions about **who you are** and **what life is** that are holding you back?*

Begin to notice when you have a strong reaction to, or an intense feeling about something. Anger, fear, sadness, depression and anxiety are all strong reactions and intense feelings that are results of conclusions and judgements. These may appear as the result of an argument, or from watching or reading a news story, or perhaps they seem to appear out of the blue. Simply begin to take notice of these feelings and know that they are there for a reason. We'll talk a lot more about how to release these as we go along, but for now, just begin to notice. **Remember:** *becoming **aware** is our goal here.*

Ask Your Body

This might seem a bit silly at first glance, but your body has the capacity to answer. Your body knows exactly where you are blocking your flow. That's its job, remember? Every answer to every question you could possibly ever ask is already contained within the cells of your body. You just have to ask, and then be willing to quiet your cognitive mind and allow the information to present itself.

Now, it is important to realize that the *body* doesn't communicate in words, but rather in feelings and emotions. Your *cognitive mind* communicates in words. So if you sit quietly and ask your body what it is trying to tell you, do not automatically look for an answer to come in words. Perhaps a scene from your past will pop into your awareness. Don't dismiss it...it is there for a reason. What key is hiding in this scenario? Look at whatever it is that comes up for you. How does it make you feel? Where do you feel that in your body? Are you experiencing an emotion as you observe the scene?

Also, don't expect the answer to reveal itself immediately, as that would be forcing the issue. The answer *may* immediately appear, but it also might take some time. Often times, your answers will appear when you least expect them: when you're taking a walk, while you're driving your car, when you're in the shower (water is a carrier of information and an amplifier of intuition) or upon awakening from sleep.

Writing your impressions down in a journal can be extremely enlightening. Don't try to analyze what you're writing. Keep your focus on the feelings and impressions you are getting from your body and write key words, small phrases, sentences or paragraphs. The style of writing is not important here, but rather allowing the information that you are currently *unaware of* to flow into your awareness. By writing it down in some fashion, the information will become 'solidly' available for you to see so you can 'turn your awareness back on' and regain clarity about your current circumstances.

Ask many questions. You'll be amazed at what information is available if you just take the time to sit quietly, ask questions and allow the information to flow in whatever form it appears.

Here are some really great questions to ask:

Dear Body, what role does (the affected body part) play for me?

Dear Body, what service is (the physical issue) providing for me?

Dear Body, what message are you trying to send me?

Dear Body, what do I need to become aware of in order to change this?

Dear Body, what (or who) do I need to let go of?

Dear Body, what habits do I need to release?

Dear Body, what type of movement do you require?

Hint: if any of these questions have a 'charge' on them for you, that's a huge indication that that is one place your flow is blocked.

Also, learning to **muscle test** can be extremely helpful when you're first learning to communicate with your body. Muscle testing, also referred to as kinesiology, can be a very accurate way of communicating with your body. The basic principle of muscle testing is that when your body is asked a yes/no-type question, the muscles will stay strong for a 'positive' response, and will weaken for a 'negative' response.

Learning to muscle test is quite easy and there are numerous methods to choose from. Doing a quick internet search for 'muscle testing' will provide multiple sites to peruse. Let's give a couple of quick and easy examples here for you to try.

Before you begin, to ensure accurate results, you might wish to drink some water to be sure your body is well hydrated, as this will enhance your body's ability to conduct energy and communicate clearly. Also, take a few deep breaths: it is very important that your mind is quiet, otherwise, your answers will be coming from your cognitive mind instead of your body. Remember: it's the *body's* response we're interested in here.

Muscle Testing Method 1. Standing

How this works: your body will naturally be drawn *forward* toward something that is *positive* and repelled *back* away from anything *negative*.

How to: Stand upright and allow your body to relax. Take a few deep, easy breaths and think of something positive, something you love...flowers, warm sunshine, fluffy puppies, cuddly kittens, love, etc. You will find that your body begins to naturally sway forward, as you are drawn toward pleasant, positive, beneficial things.

Make a true statement: My body is _____ (male/female). Your body will sway forward for statements that are *true* for you and backwards for statements that are *NOT true* for you.

Try it again. Relax your body and take a few easy breaths. Now think of something negative: war, hate, anger, cancer, destruction, etc. You will find that your body will sway backward, as it is repelled by these images. These are concepts that are contrary to the truth of the infinite Being of Love You truly are.

If you're new to muscle testing, be sure to calibrate 'yes' and 'no' by asking your body to: *show me 'YES'*...your body will lean forward; *show me 'NO'*...your body will lean back. Then, begin asking easy, obvious yes/no and true/false-type questions to which you already know the answer. This way, you and your body will being to fall in sync with each other.

Be very accurate with your questions and statements! The better the quality of your question is, or the more accurate your statement is, the better your body's response will be. *For instance:* you might make the statement, "I hate broccoli" expecting a positive (affirming) response, because you really don't enjoy eating it. However, your body gives a 'negative' response, indicating that you *like* broccoli. What happened? Well, your *body* actually likes broccoli because it has lots of good nutrition in it. *You* hate the *taste* of broccoli. It's a subtle difference, but a very important point to keep in mind. The more accurate you are, the more appropriate response you will receive.

How to Use This: You can use this method to decipher what is *appropriate, good* or *truthful* for you and your body.

Example: Before automatically taking vitamins with your morning juice, you can hold the bottle of vitamins in your hand and ask your body if it requires them right now. If you get a positive (forward) response, ask: *how many?...one?...two?...* and allow your body to give you its response. You might even consider asking if your body requires you to actually ingest the vitamins, as, by simply holding the bottle in your hand, your body will pick up on the vibrational intent of the vitamins and that might be all that is required in that moment.

Practice at the grocery store! Before *automatically* putting your 'regular' items in the basket, ask your body if it actually desires/requires them. Hold the item in your hand and ask your body if this is for your body's highest good. You might be surprised at the answers!

Practicing at the grocery store can be fun and easy! Do you want to know which cantaloupe to choose? Ask your body to pick the tastiest, ripest one and then pick them up one at a time until your body sways forward telling you to 'pick this one!' Not sure what to choose for dinner? Ask your body, "hey, body...what would be most beneficial for you for dinner tonight? Salad? Chicken? Beef? Fish?"...And don't just automatically assume that 'salad' is always supposed to be the best answer! Clear your mind, take a few deep breaths and allow your body to tell you what it requires. You might be very surprised at what it begins to tell you!

Remember: you've created illness by being unaware. This includes being unaware of what your body actually desires and requires. Do you really *enjoy* your food, or do you find yourself mindlessly eating something because *its time to eat*? What if you began eating what you *and your body* desired and required only *when* something was desired or required by you and your body? Might food taste better? Might your body respond to that food more appropriately? How might eating become a positive, fun and joyful experience for you and your body? What else is possible for you?

Muscle Testing Method 2. Using Your Fingers

This method is really quick and easy.

How This Works: Your finger muscles will remain strong for positive responses and will weaken for negative responses.

How To: Touch the tip of your ring finger (or pinky finger) to the tip of your thumb, forming a circle, sort of like making a shadow puppet bunny. Do this with each hand, making two circles. Now interlock the two circles (the bunny noses) like the links of a chain.

To muscle test, you'll *gently* pull your interlocked hands apart. For positive/true statements (or the command: show me 'yes'), your fingers will remain strong and linked together, while the link will automatically weaken and 'break' in response to negative statements (or a 'show me *no*' command).

Be sure to 'calibrate' your muscle response by having your body *show you 'yes'* (and *'no'*) and asking questions and making statements to which you are already absolutely certain of the answer. Asking simple, obvious yes/no-type questions will allow you and your body to get in sync. You want to be able to know that you are getting clear answers when you start asking questions of your body where the answers are less obvious to you, such as which actions to take and what advice to follow along your path to wellness. If you are not getting clear answers, try drinking some water, as dehydration will render your answers less accurate.

The finger method can also be done with just one hand. It is best to use your non-dominant hand, as this tends to be more accurate when you're first getting accustomed to muscle testing. Make a circle with the ring finger and your thumb, with the pad of your thumb covering the nail of your ring finger. When you ask a question or make a statement, press your finger *gently* outward against your thumb. The circle will remain strong and intact for a

42

positive/true/yes response, while your fingers will come apart and the circle will open with a negative/false/no response.

There are many different methods for muscle testing. Find the one that works the best for you, then begin to develop a working partnership with your body. Stop thinking that you automatically know what's best for your body and begin to let your body tell you what it needs and desires. Yes, salads are wonderful, but what if for today, your body actually really requires the protein from a burger? Give muscle testing a try...you might be pleased with the results!

What Part of Your Body is Involved?

Each part of your body has a very unique purpose. By looking at the purpose of the part of your body that is currently out of balance, you can get a big clue as to where your energy is blocked. Every physical issue begins with an energetic imbalance. Your physical issues are a direct reflection of where you have blocked the flow of energy.

Each body part/system performs a specific function. By examining what that function is, it is possible to see the energetic correlation. For instance, let's look at an easy example: the *eyes*. The function of the eyes is sight; the capacity to see clearly. What are you unwilling to see? Are you not liking what you see in yourself, your life or in the world? *Nearsightedness* prevents one from seeing clearly at a distance. It represents an unwillingness to see what is going on around you, an unwillingness to see the bigger picture or a resistance to seeing into the future. *Farsightedness* prevents one from seeing clearly up close. It represents an unwillingness to examine what is right in front of you, a resistance to closely examining yourself or your life.

Can you see the general correlation of eyesight issues to the energetic blockages?

Once you understand that there is a correlation between physical imbalances and energetic causes, it becomes easy to begin to uncover the patterns. Let's just compile a general list so that you can begin to see the correlations:

Arms: used for holding, carrying and hugging. Are you unwilling to embrace your life experiences? Are you not joyfully embracing life? Are you holding life at a distance? What are you resisting? Are you holding tight to something that doesn't suit you?

Back: supports the physical structure. Are you feeling unsupported? Is there something going on behind your back that you need to become aware of? Are you not proud of yourself (standing tall and proud)?

Bladder: collects and releases urine. What are you holding onto? What are you afraid of letting go? What are you pissed off about?

Breasts: nurture and supply nourishment. Do you take the time to nurture yourself? Do you allow yourself to receive nourishment from others? Are you refusing to flow energy to someone?

Circulatory System: provides blood flow to nourish the cellular structure. What has limited your ability to go with the flow? What is inhibiting your ability to move freely, fluidly and joyfully with the flow of life?

Colon: removal of waste. Are you holding onto 'stuff' from your past? What are you refusing to let pass?

Heart: represents love. Do you love yourself? Do you allow yourself to receive love? Do you need to forgive yourself or someone else? Where have you decided that you can only love one person at a time? Where have you decided that love looks exactly like *this* and not like *that*? Do you realize that the entire fabric of the universe *is* Love? Do you realize that you *are* Love?

Immune System: keeps the body cleansed, strong and balanced by clearing out infections. Are you feeling weak and vulnerable to attack? Unable to defend/stand up for yourself? What energies must be cleared out (guilt, shame, unworthiness, etc.) in order to bring yourself back into strength and balance?

Knees: are the flexible part of the leg. They have to do with strength, flexibility and humility (on bended knee). Where have you become inflexible? Where have you stuck energy in a box (i.e., *this* is what it needs to look like) and therefore restricted your flexibility? Where are you invested in being *right? Where are you being not good enough? Where are you being superior?*

Legs: used for support and transportation. Resistance to, or fear of, moving forward. Feeling unstable, unsupported, unsure about taking next step.

Lungs: represent the breath of life; the connection to Source. The inability to be at one with your Inner Being. Where have you separated yourself from Source? Do you feel unworthy? Are you willing to remember the Grand Being You Are?

Reproductive System: used for sexual expression and creation of life. Are you able to freely and safely express your desires, your needs and your creativity? Are you suppressing your powers of creation and creativity? Are your masculine (power) and feminine (creativity) energies in balance?

Shoulders: provide freedom of movement to the arms. Are you carrying the weight of the world on your shoulders? What is weighing heavily on you and limiting your freedom, joy and ability to embrace life?

Stomach: used for digestion. The ability to effortlessly digest life. What ideas or experiences are hard to digest?

Uterus: creates/births new life. Are you expressing your creativity? What new ideas or creations are waiting for you to give them life?

Once you discover that there is a correlation between body parts and energetic causes of imbalances, it becomes much easier to uncover the patterns that are blocking your well-being.

Also, remember to talk to your body!

Ask the body part what message it has for you.

Ask what job it is performing for you.

Ask what *service* the 'condition' you are experiencing is providing...because, believe it or not, it *is* serving you! Perhaps your stomach is trying to protect you, or your sacrum is trying to get you to slow down and focus within, or the systemic infection is *asking for permission* to change. You might be very surprised at the messages your body will give to you, if you will only listen!

What are you Focusing on?

Let's take a look at the overview of your daily life. Feel into a typical day. What energy do you feel? Do you feel happy or sad? Do you feel stress or ease? Do you feel heavy or light? Yes, you can feel all of these things in any one day, but we're talking about in general... the overall energy of your life as it stands today. In general, let's take an energetic snapshot of your life. What do you see? How do you feel inside your body? Keep this picture in mind for a moment.

In order to release blocked energy from your body, you'll need to become aware of patterns that you've developed. If you've gotten in the habit of focusing on *what's wrong with me*, you'll need to change that in order to change your health. Remember: your body must reflect your thoughts and beliefs back to you, so if you're focusing on *what's wrong with me*...your body will need to provide you with an answer!

This reality teaches us that *IT* is *real* and that we are simply *responding* to reality as it is presented to us. This is NOT true! *We create* our reality through our focus. What we believe...we see reflected back to us.

Because we have been trained to believe that we are simply *reacting to* reality, rather than *creating it,* we have developed the habit of looking at what *IS* and then judging what we see. If we see something that we don't like, we have a negative reaction. We FEEL that negative reaction, and that impacts our cellular structure. If we continually have negative reactions to this reality, we are continually bombarding our cellular structure with negative or toxic energy.

In order to improve our health, we must improve the quality of input we are sending to our cellular structure. We need to move our focus away from the negative *what is*, and develop a new, positive input from the *vision* of what we *choose.*

What would you like your life to feel like?

What?

Yes...if you could *feel* any way you choose, what would you choose to feel? If you were *being* your true Soul Self, what would that feel like? What would it feel like to be your Soul? Would it feel happy? Light? Free? At ease? What would you choose? Think about your ideal life...life on YOUR terms...life the way you'd like it to be. If you could create anything you desired...any life you desired... any state of health...what would *that* feel like?

Now, let's go back to that energetic snapshot of the overall picture of your life you took a minute ago. What does *that* picture *feel* like? Do you notice a difference between these two scenarios? Is there a difference between the current snapshot and the dream?

The snapshot of your life as it feels today, is the snapshot of the quality of energy you are currently focused on. Is this the quality of energy that you desire? If not, then you'll need to re-focus.

How do I do that?

Well, you'll need to *choose*. First, you'll need to *choose* what it is that you'd like to experience. Then you'll need to *choose* to find things to focus on that match that energy. Then, you'll need to choose to become aware of when you're focusing in the opposite direction of what you desire, then you'll need to choose to re-focus on the quality of energy you desire. You see, saying that you desire to change is great, but that's just lip service. In order to change anything in your life, you need to make a clear CHOICE. *Choice is empowerment.*

Remember how we chose *playful* and *happy?* You can choose any state of being you desire, simply by placing your attention on it! If you'd like your body or your life to feel differently that it does, you'll have to first *feel differently*...intend to feel differently, then focus your attention on that feeling.

Listen to your self talk. What is the general tone of your daily conversations? Where is your focus? What do you tell yourself on a daily basis? Do you judge yourself? Do you judge others? Do you gossip?

In order to change a negative circumstance into a positive one, you must change your negative talk into positive, empowering conversation with yourself as well as with others. Start to pay attention to your words and your energies. Take notice of when you're using negative words and energies. Notice when you are being critical of yourself or others. Criticizing yourself or others, or telling stories of ailments or failings will *not* help...it will work against you!

Do you choose vibrant, radiant health? Then you're going to have to create ways to *feel* that each day. You'll want to have vibrant, radiant conversations with yourself and others. You'll need to find positive words to use that will make both you and others feel empowered and happy.

Focus on what you desire, not on what *is*. Because this reality teaches us that *it* is real and that we are reacting to *it*, we come to believe that what we see IS because it IS. This is not true. What we see is the *result* of what we have created in the PAST. In order to change what IS, we need to focus on what we choose to create.

This is not to say to ignore or deny the current situation, but rather to *accept* what IS and *focus* on what you choose to create. You cannot get to *vibrant, radiant health* by focusing on *poor me*, but you *can* get there from *I've created this undesirable condition, and now I'm choosing something different.*

Start telling a better quality story. If you keep *telling it like it is*...then you just keep creating the same thing over and over and nothing can change because you're keeping it locked in place. In order to change *what IS*...you have to start telling a different story. You have to change your point of awareness. If you're speaking from the point of view that *I have this condition*...then you have to continue to *have that condition* because you're telling the universe that you *have that condition*. In order to change the condition, you have to come from the point of view that you are *choosing health*.

If you desire to create a better life story for yourself, you'll have to stop telling the old story. You'll have to start telling a more empowering story for yourself. You'll need to find ways to start telling the story that you would like to live. Would you be willing to let go of your story? Would you be willing to release your past in lieu of creating your future? Would you be willing to tell a completely *new* story? What new story would you like to tell?

Section Three:
Disease:
Deeper Truths

Facing the Disease

Is it Someone Else's?
What?

That's right...is it really *your* disease...or...is it actually someone else's reality that you just assumed must be your reality, too? Did your mother have breast cancer, so now you have it, too? Does kidney disease 'run in your family', so now it's *your* turn? Are your 'bad knees' just like your father's bad knees? Did you get *your mother's* premature gray hair or *your father's* poor eyesight?

This is a pervasive misconception of the Third Dimension. *Diseases* DO NOT *run in the family*...**undesirable 'belief system programming'** *does!*

Yes...you read that correctly. And, yes...it flies directly in the face of everything your doctors have ever told you. And, yes...this reality (i.e., the hologram of physicality) appears to offer indisputable *proof* that 'diseases run in the family.'

So...here we stand...

Are we standing 'on the horns of a dilemma?' Is this just crazy-talk? Or, are we looking at a huge opportunity to change our entire reality?

Which do you choose? *Dilemma* or opportunity for change? What does your inner knowing tell you about this?

49

Could we have inadvertently been buying into a *lie* for our whole lives up until now? Is your current reality so amazing and wonderful that you will fight to keep it locked in place by continuing to defend this belief?

Or, what if you could change your entire reality into something that actually *worked* for you, simply by addressing and changing this set of beliefs?

What if *both* sets of beliefs are TRUE? Can two seemingly contradictory beliefs *both* be true? Which belief feels most expansive? Which one feels *most* true for you? Which do you *choose?*

Are you willing to explore this a little further? Okay. Let's break this down.

Physical reality is designed for unlimited Beings (*us!*) to be able to explore themselves within the parameters of limitation. In our *natural* state of being, we experience ourselves as completely *un*limited. We have no judgements of good and bad, right and wrong...everything simply falls into the category of *experience.*

As humans inside the Third Dimension, we experience ourselves as *finite* and *limited.* We judge all of our experiences as either good or bad or right or wrong (duality). By judging our experiences, we place our experiences in 'boxes' of limitation, labeling the boxes as either desirable or undesirable.

When we place energy in boxes, we stop the natural flow of the energies. When energy gets trapped inside our cellular structure, we manifest physical symptoms.

So, from the *limited human* perspective, we believe that we are susceptible to germs, viruses and diseases. We've been taught, and have learned from experience *from inside the box of this limited reality,* that diseases 'run in the family' and therefore this is a true statement...from within the confines of Third Dimensional reality. Science has proven it...just ask your favorite physician or ask the one who is experiencing the 'family disease.'

Because our bodies are always reflecting our beliefs, judgements and conclusions back to us, if we carry beliefs that say we're prone to disease, then our bodies have to reflect that back to us. Therefore, because this reality teaches us that these beliefs are true, we buy into these beliefs as truth and the beliefs are then made manifest in our bodies. We then use the physical manifestation as *proof* that our belief is true, which then keeps the belief locked in place in our realities.

However, from *outside* the Third Dimension, from our natural, unlimited nature, there is only flow and harmony. Within *flow* and *harmony*, disease cannot exist.

Any disease that is experienced within the physical body stems from a belief that is contrary to the flow of well-being. The one who experiences disease has simply bought into a belief system that dictates that disease either can, or will be, experienced and then this reality, responding accordingly, has reflected that belief back through the physicalized experience.

From outside the Third Dimension, it is understood that a disease cannot be 'inherited,' but the *belief systems* involving physical disease *can* be adopted. So if you can switch your perspective from *3-D limited human* to *5-D Expanded Being*, then you can easily see through this paradigm.

It's the belief-system programming that causes the diseases, the diseases don't just show up by themselves. (Remember: everything originates as a thought before it is manifest in the physical.) Can you now start to see how *diseases* don't 'run in the family' but *undesirable belief-system programming* DOES? So…what do you do now?

If you choose to continue to believe that disease can be inherited, then you must adhere to the rules of this reality and allow the disease to play itself out within the normal parameters of physical reality.

If, however, you choose to remember your *unlimited* nature, you can now remove the limiting belief structures you've placed upon your experience of reality, and allow your body to realign with the natural flow of well-being, similar to removing a dam that has been stopping up the flow of a river.

Which truth do you choose?

Disease–What is it Really?
Hint: There is nothing to fear!

Cancer. AIDS. Diabetes. Heart Disease. The mere sight of these words can be enough to strike fear into the hearts of the ones who have been diagnosed along with their families and friends. Would you be willing to release that fear?

Let's look at disease from a new perspective and see if we can drain all the power out of 'disease', and return all of that power back to you. Are you willing to take a journey into the face of disease, look it in the eye, *let it go* and reclaim your power?

Is that even possible?

YES! How do I know? Because I already did it! And if *I* can do it, so can *you!*

If you're willing to be brave…come with me and let's explore. Let's see if we can de-bunk this 'disease thing' once and for all and let it vanish from your life as it vanished from mine. Are you ready? Let's go…

Let's use the example of *cancer* because it is so prevalent. It has permeated all levels of society and it 'strikes' in many different forms. Cancer is our example, but this is true for any disease.

Okay. So we have already established that your body's job is to directly reflect all of your thoughts and beliefs back to you, and we've also determined that you are an Infinite Being whose natural state is that of well-being. Cancer, therefore, (or any other disease, for that matter) is simply your body's way of telling you that you have pinched off the flow of well-being.

'Cancer' is a term that the medical community has used to describe certain sets of symptoms, usually indicating that cells have 'gone rogue' and have started multiplying uncontrollably, apparently 'attacking' you, the victim. Over the years, the term has come to embody the energies of fear, of death, of victimhood and suffering. A LOT of energy has been embedded into it. The mere sound of the word sends shivers of dread into the one who has been diagnosed.

We have come to believe that *Cancer* 'attacks its victims' and therefore we have given *cancer* a 'persona'…an individual identity… and it has come to be perceived as an 'enemy.' It is seen as a huge, dark 'entity' that comes on the attack to steal lives and cause physical and emotional pain for its victims and their loved ones. It is like an army of grief, death and destruction. No wonder everyone feels the need to 'fight' cancer!

However, is this actually true? What is really happening?

Well, what's really happening is that your body is telling you that you have fallen out of alignment with your true nature. You have a 'kink in the hose' that is preventing your natural well-being from flowing freely. That is all.

Cancer (or any other malady) is simply your body sending you a message. Your body is the physical extension of YOU, so this cancer is really just *You* sending *You* a message.

It is saying, "Dear Self: do you hate yourself/your life so much that you are trying to kill yourself? Have you forgotten how to love yourself? Have you buried your joy? It is time to remember the incredible, infinite Being of Love and Joy that You Are. You *are* a *Well* Being! Are you willing to remember how precious you really are and how much fun life can actually be? Are you ready to reclaim the Well Being *You Are?*"

Your dear, precious body is NOT trying to kill you. It loves you...heck, it *is* You! It desires to live! Do you think that your body would rather be healthy or diseased? Your body has no 'hidden agenda' to cause you grief...it actually loves you unconditionally. Your body is serving you in every moment. Its job (which You assigned to it) is to directly reflect your beliefs back to you and it is performing its task to perfection!

So where did I block the flow?

The first place to look is: *hatred*. (Cancer has come to represent the enemy; we hate our enemies.) Do you hate something about yourself or your life? Do you hate who or what you've become? Do you hate this reality? Are you unlovable? Are you carrying around guilt, shame, blame or unforgiveness of yourself or another, allowing it to 'eat away' at your body? Would you rather die than forgive yourself or another? Are you unworthy?

The next place to look is: *powerlessness*. (Cancer appears to be a mighty, powerful enemy that has come to attack the vulnerable.) Do you believe that you are a victim? Have you given up your innate power? Do you believe you are weak or vulnerable? Do you believe life is unfair? Do 'good guys always finish last?'

For any disease, step back and look at the bigger energetic picture to get an idea of where you have blocked the flow. For example: *diabetes* is an imbalance in blood sugar. Sugar is a sweetener. Where are you refusing to embrace the sweetness of life?

Remember: You are an Infinite Being. The word *Infinite* means just that: infinite; unlimited; all-encompassing. *You are Well-Being Itself* experiencing yourself within the confines of physicality. An Infinite Being *encompasses* ALL energies. If You encompass *all energies,* are there any energies that you are *not*? No! So, are there any energies that you need to fear? Of course not! Why would you fear something that you *are*? This *disease* is just another aspect of... *You! **There is no need to fear Yourself!!!***

Would you be willing to allow all *disease* to dissolve into nothingness in the face of the reality that your body is temporarily out of balance? Would you be willing to allow cancer to *not be* cancer? Would you be willing to allow cancer to stop existing? Would you be willing to allow *all diseases* to cease to exist in lieu of a *temporary physical imbalance?*

Is this too radically simplistic to consider?

Is cancer a much too serious subject to be treated so 'lightly'?

I am able to ask these questions because I have already experienced this for myself and I can attest that I literally allowed disease to dissolve from my life. Once I realized that the disease was MY BODY sending ME a message...that it was ME...that the 'cancer' was ME...I stopped being afraid of it. I realized that there was absolutely no reason to fear mySelf. I had been giving my power over to the condition by feeding it with my fear. I had made the disease bigger and more powerful than Me. The moment that I realized that 'disease' was not really 'disease' (as a separate entity)...it was really just ME...the entire concept of *disease* instantly vanished. The lumps and bumps and physical symptoms literally began dissolving from my body because they no longer existed as 'disease' in my awareness. I realized that 'disease' is an illusion...it is not an independent entity...it is simply the body sending a message!

The moment I realized this, I immediately reclaimed my power from it. I saw how I had been feeding it with my fear...so I instantly stopped feeding it and I *pulled my power back to me.* I realized that I had been 'duped' by an illusion, and I *called my energy back* and reclaimed the Well Being I Am.

I realized that all 'disease' boils down to one thing: *my body is out of balance because I've fallen out of alignment with my*

Inner Well-Being. Period. *As I re-align with the Truth of my Inner Being, my body comes back into balance.* It really is that simple.

As long as you choose to view any disease as *serious* or *life-threatening*, you are giving power to the disease and you are feeding the condition with your fear. Is this what you really wish to choose? Do you really desire for the disease to have power over you?

Would you be willing to take back your power, allow the concept of the disease as an *entity* to dissolve, and then allow your body to begin to rebalance itself as you release the distortions in your belief system that are distorting your natural well-being? (Your body has the ability to rebalance itself built right into it, by the way.) Or would that be much too simple to actually work? Would you be willing to allow all disease to dissolve from your reality? Would you allow radiant health to be your natural state of existence? What would your life be like if disease didn't exist in your world?

This is now my reality. Disease doesn't exist in my world. Yes, I see others in *dis*-ease around me and I am aware of how very *real* their *experience* is for them, as I have been there, too. However, I also now realize that a totally different choice is available for everyone. That is why I have written this book: to share my experience and insights and show others that there is a completely different reality that is available to be experienced by any and all who are willing to choose it.

Once I realized that the *disease* was Me, and that I was creating the imbalance by blocking the flow of well-being, I chose to re-open the flow by focusing on the health and well-being that is My *natural* state of Being. I realized that physical dis-ease is contrary to our natural state...it is a distortion of our natural *ease*...our natural harmony and balance. Once I realized this, I began to focus on my *inherent* well-Being. I realized that well-Being is Who I Am...it is my core essence. I then began to *know* my way back to radiant health. I *knew* that my Being is naturally radiantly healthy and balanced. The places where I had been blocking the flow then began to become apparent, and I saw them for the distortions they were.

I began to see where I was being untrue to the infinite Being I Am. I began to see where I had been resenting life, making myself 'less than' and giving my power away. As I saw the distortions and recognized that they were contrary to Who I Am...to what my Soul Is, they began to simply fall away and my body began to return to its natural state of ease and radiant health.

The body is a self-healing and self-rebalancing entity. If left to its own devices in its natural state (without all of our limiting beliefs mucking it up!), it will automatically heal and rebalance itself. It is just our own cognitive distortions that prevent the body from experiencing radiant health. If we are judging ourselves, hating ourselves, denying ourselves, disrespecting ourselves and generally cutting off the flow of love to ourselves, it will show up in our bodies (or in our bank accounts or in our relationships) in one form or another.

Once we realize that radiant health is inherent...it is how we are *designed*...we can choose that as our platform. We can realize that radiant health is *who we are* and we can then begin to let go of the patterns of limiting beliefs we are holding onto so that we can allow our natural state of health and vitality to flow through our bodies once more.

I will go even one step further. In addition to allowing cancer to dissolve from my reality, I have actually become *grateful* for my experience! Can you imagine being grateful for your health challenge? I have profound gratitude for my experience, because without going through it, I would never have developed the level of awareness I now possess. It was a pivotal experience that I have used to set myself free.

Would you be willing to let disease dissolve from your reality? Are you willing to choose a radiantly healthy life? Are you willing to reclaim *your* power and set *yourself* free?

Stop Fighting the Disease

This brings up another key factor in the healing paradigm: you must stop **fighting** diseases. By *fighting*, you are keeping the very thing that you are fighting against locked in place.

Say what?!

Yes! By *fighting* (either *for* or *against*) anything...whether it be cancer, poverty, war, animal cruelty or any other cause...you are unwittingly keeping the very thing you are fighting with locked into your reality.

What are you talking about?! I'm fighting for my life over here! You want me to just give up?

NO!...and YES! This is a very important piece of the puzzle that you must fully understand in order to empower yourself and begin to create your life from the platform of your own choosing:

If you are either fighting *for* your life or *against* a disease, then you are believing that something is a threat to your life. As an Infinite Being, there is *nothing* that can harm you...ever. So let's see if we can look at *fighting* in a different light.

We have just determined that any *disease* is not an entity unto itself, therefore it is also not a 'killer' that needs to be fought. By fighting against it, you are turning it into an entity and you are feeding it with your energy. YOU are *giving your power over to IT.* You are turning your physical imbalance into an 'enemy' and you are 'feeding' that enemy with your focused attention.

Do you really wish to continue to feed your enemy? If you stop feeding something, what happens to it? What happens to your houseplants when you stop watering them? Would you be willing to stop watering the experiences that you don't want?

Let's see if we can use a silly metaphor here that might make this really simple to see. Let's say that you go to a buffet at a nice restaurant. It is a huge spread...hundreds of items to choose from. It is a grand feast for both the eyes and the stomach. You take your plate and head to the island of delectable delights. You see all the beautiful foods to choose from...ahhh...such a wonderful creation!

Until...right there...right in the middle of all the other beautiful offerings...*beets!*

"I hate beets!" you shout. *"My mother hates beets, my grandmother hates beets...I come from a long line of beet haters! Beets are horrible! Those beets are going to jump onto my plate and ruin my entire dinner! We have to eradicate all beets! Someone get over here and remove these beets!"*

By now, you've begun to attract some attention! Some people may be whispering in your ear, quietly telling you stop making a scene. Others, who also don't enjoy beets, may be supporting your efforts to have them removed from the table. Some people might be shouting from their tables at you to sit down and shut up. The manager might be trying to calm you down.

All the while, the poor innocent beets are just...*there*. They are simply BEing a choice. Some people love them, some people hate them and others have no real opinion one way or the other.

Do you see how your *reaction* to the beets caused the commotion...the beets themselves really had nothing at all to do with it?

Do you see that when you **feast at the banquet of life** you can choose the items that *please* you and you can simply *leave the rest alone* for someone else to choose?

Do you see that although you may not desire to eat beets, there are plenty of other people who love them? Are the people who love them *bad* people? Are they *wrong* for enjoying them? Do you need to start campaigns *against* beets and people who enjoy them?

What do you think would happen to the beets if no one ever chose them again? Do you think that the restaurant would continue to offer them if no one *ever* chose them? Do you see that as long as people are still choosing the beets, they are serving a purpose and they will remain on the table?

Do you see that focused attention on the **unwanted** item took a lot of energy, caused a big commotion and got many other people involved?

Do you see that when feasting from the banquet of life...you don't have to *fight against* the items you don't desire...you can simply choose the ones you like!

What might your life be like if you no longer *fought against* anything?

What might your life be like if you *stopped fighting* what you *don't* want, and started *focusing on* your desires?

What if you stopped trying to *convince others?*

What if you stopped *fighting* your physical imbalance and started *feeding* your **innate well-being**? Would you be willing to *stop fighting* and *start living* the life You *choose?*

You see, for me...the disease (the beets) was actually serving a purpose. I chose my disease (albeit unwittingly...through my unawareness)...but by 'choosing' the disease...it propelled me into greater knowingness and it actually served to set me free. I'm now *grateful* for my experience. Would anyone logically suspect that any disease was actually serving a higher purpose? No! Of course not! However, I'm grateful that it was a 'choice on the buffet table'...because unbeknownst to me at the time...it was the key to my freedom.

Would you be willing to stop *fighting* cancer, AIDS, diabetes, arthritis (or any other disease) and allow it to be simply another choice on the buffet table of life, or even the key to your (or someone else's) freedom?

What if, instead of *fighting* diseases, you simply allowed the disease to dissolve from your reality by focusing on your inherent well-Being? What if you could then show others how to do the same thing? If everyone knew how to dissolve disease from their reality, would there still be a need to fight diseases? Or would it become possible for people to 'not choose' the diseases and simply choose their own natural, radiant health and vitality? What does your Inner Knowing tell you about this?

LIFE...Will You Choose It?

This brings us to another key concept: *choosing life*. This is often overlooked, because of course you don't want to *die!* But hear this clearly: **not wanting to die is definitely NOT the same thing as choosing to LIVE!**

If you are experiencing a 'grave' condition, that is exactly where you're allowing the disease to take you...to the grave. What are you *dying* to get away from? Are you *sick* of your life?

Disease is like a slow-acting *escape button* from this reality! It is the 'button' you push that gives you the option of escaping from the story you've created for this lifetime through the process of 'death.' It's actually a wonderful thing, because it ensures that we return ourselves to balance! *Yes!* Either we address the cause of the imbalance and return ourselves to our natural health and balance *in* our body, or, we *leave* the body and return to balance in the non-physical realms...so that we can then turn right around and give it another go...because we have such fun creating these illusions! Either way, we return to balance. So you see, you can't make a mistake!

So...if you're experiencing disease, you've given yourSelf a choice: do you wish to *escape this reality* or do you choose to *live?* The good news here is that you can't make the *wrong* choice! This reality teaches us that death is *bad*...that it would be the *wrong choice*. But in light of the fact that You are an Infinite Being, you really *cannot* 'die'...it's impossible! You *can* lay this body down and return to the *unlimited, non-physical Being* You *are*...but then those who remain 'behind' in bodies would be *sad* and that would be *bad*...so you'd better resist *dying*...but you're already resisting *living*...so hmmm...it seems that you might be facing a conundrum!

But what if there was ANOTHER choice?

What if you could choose to LIVE?! ...Not just *'survive'*, but really *LIVE?!*

What if you could choose a life that you'd be really *excited* about? Would it be worth sticking around for a life that really *worked* for you...in a body that was vibrantly healthy? Would you be willing to consider that option?

Did you know that this reality is designed to respond to your every command? Did you know that once you make a **clear choice**...that the Universe begins to rearrange itself to reflect your choice back to you?!

Have you actually *chosen* to *live*...or have you just been trying to avoid death?

Would you be willing to make a **clear choice**...and then allow the universe to begin to rearrange itself for you?

Victim/Perpetrator Paradigm

Let's explore the 'Cancer game'...or any other *disease game* or *physical limitation game*...you might be currently choosing.

Inside the world of Duality, we explore contrast and opposites. There are winners and losers, geniuses and idiots, athletes and weaklings, etc. Woven into this 'disease game' is a very interesting paradigm of opposites called *Victim and Perpetrator*, which, if seen clearly, can completely stop the *disease game* in its tracks.

Do you believe that you are a **victim** of your disease?

Sure!

Okay...so, since the disease was created within the confines of duality, if there is a *victim* there must also be a *perpetrator*, because duality is based upon interconnected opposites. So who is the victim and who is the perpetrator in your scenario? "That's

60

obvious," you say..."I'm the victim and the Cancer is the perpetrator." ...*Wrong!*

What?!

The cancer is *not* an entity unto itself. Humans have personified it as 'the enemy,' however, it is not an entity unto itself and therefore it is not capable of being an *enemy*. It has no agenda. It is simply how the cells of your body are sending you a specific message. It cannot be a perpetrator.

Hmmm...okay...but...I'm still the victim, right?

Right!

Okay, good!...No, wait...okay...let me get this straight...I'm the victim, but the cancer is not the perpetrator?

Correct!

Really? Then who is?

Well...are you ready for this? The perpetrator is...*You!*

Say what?!?

Yes, you read that right: You are the victim *and* the perpetrator!

Holy cow! How can that be?

Pretty tricky, huh?

Okay, here's how this works: the *victim* part is obvious...it appears as if you, the innocent bystander, has been attacked by this cancer. That's easy to see. The flip side of that coin, however, is not quite as obvious. You are the perpetrator because you are the creator of the disease in the first place!

Remember: You create your own reality. You did not create this on purpose...you created it through unawareness, but nonetheless *You* are the creator. We have come into this physical reality to explore duality...both sides of the same coin. So, if you believe that there are victims, then there must also be perpetrators. Usually we think of these as two separate individuals, which is why, since we're obviously the victims, we would never even think that we could also be the perpetrators!

What a grand illusion we have created! Do you see what an incredible feat this is? You are the victim of...*Yourself!*

Can you see the illusion? Your body got out of balance, you called it a disease and tried to fight against the disease. However, we've already established that the disease is simply *You sending a message to Yourself*...so, by fighting your disease, *you're only fighting yourself!* Pretty wild, huh?

Do you see what this means? Within the infinite scope of the All-That-Is, You are such a *grand, powerful Creator* that you have succeeded in experiencing yourself as each side of the same coin independently, while *being* the coin itself! Wow! *That's really amazing!* Congratulations!

You have succeeded in 'forgetting' your infinite power by 'feeding' your power into a 'disease' that is an illusion, making that illusion more powerful than You, causing yourself to suffer, while at the same time...all of it is...*You! Holy cow!*

Do you realize that the only way that cancer (or any other disease) can even exist is if we continue to believe in it and feed it with our focused attention? As long as we continue to feed it, it will continue to exist and victimize us. By feeding it with our energies, we are making it more powerful than we are. We are *INFINITE Beings*...there is *nothing* that is *MORE powerful* than Us! *It is impossible!* There is no other entity in All of Creation that is *MORE* powerful (or *less* powerful) than You!...It would throw the entirety of All of Creation out of whack and that, too, is impossible!

Now, would you be willing to reclaim your power and become your own Savior and stop playing this game? Would you be willing to intervene on your own behalf and stop playing your own victim and perpetrator? Would you be willing to recognize that your body is simply out of balance...that it has been following the orders that you have *unconsciously* been giving it? Would you be willing to become *conscious* about the health you choose? Would you be willing to *consciously choose* vibrant, radiant health and then allow your body to rebalance itself by *consciously* allowing the natural flow of well-being? Would you be willing to ask your body to start guiding you back into balance?

Side Note: after struggling through my experience, the moment I saw that the disease was not an entity and therefore could not be the perpetrator...that *I* was my own perpetrator *and* victim...I laughed hysterically...as I knew that the 'jig was up!' I saw so clearly what I had done and I saw that the 'joke was on *ME!*' All of the fear went away and I saw what an incredible job my dear body had done to reflect all of my belief systems back to me! I had a completely new respect and admiration for my sweet body! I had spent so long *resisting* and *resenting* my body for being unhealthy...I finally saw that my body was simply doing exactly what I was programming it to do! Thank you, body!

I then made the very *clear choice* to stop playing that 'victim/perpetrator game.' I said *NO MORE... I CHOOSE LIFE*...and the game was over.

Your Body: from Resentment to Appreciation

This brings us to another point: would you be willing to *stop resenting* your dear body? The fact that it is out of balance is *NOT* your body's fault! Your body *loves* you! Your body *desires* to be vitally healthy and in balance...it desires to LIVE! The current imbalance you are experiencing in your body is the result of some 'bad programming' that is running through your system.

This reality, by design (we're exploring *Limitation*, remember?), programs us to believe that we are small, insignificant, separate and limited. We believe that we have no control...that we are tossed about upon a sea of destiny. There are winners and losers and some folks are just lucky. We believe that we are susceptible to germs and diseases. Look at that one for a moment: we believe that something so tiny as a germ...that is only visible with the aid of a high-powered microscope...can kill an Infinite Being! Is that actually true? What does your knowingness tell you about that?

So you've been programmed by this reality that all kinds of bad stuff happens to bodies...fat, wrinkles, hair growing where you don't want it, no hair growing where you do want it, aches, pains and diseases...and our poor bodies have the job of reflecting those disempowering belief systems back to us! Our bodies love us so much that they sacrifice their natural well-being for our benefit!

The aches, pains and imbalances that we experience through our bodies are actually our bodies way of communicating to us... we just haven't been listening! Every ache, pain or imbalance...is our body's way of sending us information! It's our body asking us: *are you sure you want to hold on to that disempowering belief?...Are you ready to let that go yet?* No?...*(...a little twinge)...Are you ready to let that go yet?* No?...*(..a bigger twinge)...Are you ready to let that go yet?* Still *No?...(..a pain)...ARE YOU READY TO LET THAT GO YET?...(..a full-blown imbalance).*

So...are you ready to let go of some of those worn-out beliefs? Are you willing to accept that you are the Grand, Infinite Being that You Are and let go of the limiting beliefs you *bought into* through the programming of this reality? Are you ready to 'remove your veil', turn your *awareness* back on and allow your dear body to return to its natural vitality?

Would you be willing to acknowledge that your body is NOT your enemy?

Would you be willing to allow your body to be your best friend? Would you allow *You* to be your own best friend?

What would it be like if you actually *loved* your body? What would it be like if you actually *loved* your Self?

I wonder what would happen if you actually *loved* being in your body...if you were able to really *appreciate* what an incredible, miraculous vehicle your body truly is...I wonder what life would be like then...

Would you be willing to develop a new relationship with your body? Would you allow yourself to develop a *friendship* with your body? Would you allow your body to help you create a *life* that really *works?*

Would you be willing to acknowledge that your body is worthy of your love and respect? Would you be willing to acknowledge that YOU are worthy of your love and respect?

Would you be willing to acknowledge that your body is ready, willing and able to rebalance itself *right now*...and that it just needs your permission? Would you be willing to give your body permission?

Which would you prefer: the feeling of *resentment* or the feeling of *appreciation?*

Do you realize that you can choose to feel that with your body *right now?*

How do you begin to appreciate your body?

First, you must realize that your body is *not* the enemy...it is *not* sabotaging your life.

Then realize that it is playing the exact role that *you* designed for it. It is showing you exactly what your beliefs are. Change your limiting beliefs and your body will change.

Would you be willing to go *beyond beliefs*...and allow your body to help you remember what Your Soul *knows?* Would you be willing to *get rid of your beliefs* and tap into your true KNOWING by letting your body lead you?

Would you consider giving your body a hug? Yes...an actual hug! Would you be willing to give your body a hug and say 'hello'?

When was the last time you said a simple hello to your body?

Go ahead...give your body a hug and say hello...see what happens...we won't tell anyone!

Would you be willing to apologize to it for resenting it...and making it distort itself for your benefit...when you couldn't even see the benefit?

What if a simple *hug* and a sincere *hello* to your body on a daily basis could change your life? Would you be willing to give it a try?

If you'd like to try something a little more advanced, you could add a *Thank you* or an *I love You* to the hug and the hello. But don't rush right into that...that's only for experts!

SECTION FOUR:

Returning to Health...
Clearing the Blocks

Look It Directly in the Eye

Taking full responsibility is the quickest way to release anything that is holding you in discomfort.

What does that mean?

It means to take responsibility for creating your current condition, because anything that *you* created, *you* can also un-create. It means to *acknowledge* the situation for what it is: *you've created* an imbalance...an indication that you have shut off your awareness in some area. *Accept* that you've been wearing the 'veil of forgetfulness' and have temporarily forgotten that you are an Infinite Being...*oops! Choose* that it's now time to turn your awareness back on, *remember* that health and balance are *natural* for You, and begin to allow the condition to rebalance itself. It doesn't have to be a great big deal...unless you choose for it to be.

If you insist that it can't possibly be that simple...then you are arguing for your limitations. You are saying that this imbalance is real...it can't easily change...it has to be a difficult process. Is that what you truly desire? What if it *could* be simple? What if it's not *nearly* as difficult as you've been taught to believe?

Taking full responsibility for your current situation and accepting it, will allow it to change, while *denying* and *resisting* will keep it locked in place. You'll want to be certain to become aware of any place you're in denial or resistance.

You *cannot* change anything that you wish to change about yourself or your situation through *denial* or *resistance (believe me...I tried!)*. If you *deny* that you are the creator of your condition or deny that you even *have* the condition, then you are not taking full responsibility for yourself. By not taking responsibility, you are giving your power away and creating yourself as a victim. *Responsibility* is the ability to respond. You are a grand, powerful Being of Magnitude...you are infinitely capable of taking control of the situation and allowing it to transform.

Resistance keeps things locked in place by *pushing against* what is unwanted. As you resist, you feed your power to whatever you are resisting by focusing your attention on it. Have you heard the saying that *what you resist, persists?* It's true.

The opposite of resistance is acceptance. Acceptance does not mean that you have to *like* it...it simply means that you have to accept that it *IS*. It is the acceptance that you've created it...and now you are ready to create it differently. You created it through unawareness, it is what it is, but now you're ready to allow it to change through your expanded awareness.

So how do I acknowledge and accept this?

In order to accept something, you must STOP trying to push it away or deny it (think of our *beets*). Pushing against anything only keeps you stuck. It's like trying to paddle against the flow of the river. If you're pushing against (resisting) the flow, you have to work very hard, you don't go far and eventually you become exhausted. Acceptance is hopping into your kayak and guiding yourself down the river (allowing the beets to simply be there while you choose something else).

Well-being is the flow of the universe! Going with the flow... the flow of universal energy...will not get you smashed upon the rocks if you are being aware. By becoming aware of your *Inner Knowing* and even asking for angelic assistance, the natural flow of the universe will allow you to guide yourself into the soft, steady flow of well being that is your natural state.

See Your Dis-ease for What it Really Is:
A Miraculous Achievement!

What?!?

Yes...it's actually the mark of success!

No way!...How do you figure that?!

Well...the truth is that you are an Infinite, Unlimited Being. You volunteered to come to Earth and play this game of Limitation. You put the veil over your head and forgot who You Are...*MISSION ACCOMPLISHED! Good job! You are a success!*

Now...would you be willing to accept that you are a *grand success* and that you have accomplished what you came here to accomplish? You've experienced the lack and limitation that you intended to experience! The undesirable condition is not a horrible, ugly monster that is real and unchangeable, it is just the means by which you've been exploring limitation!

Would you be willing to lift your veil, remember Who You Are, and allow YourSelf to return to the vibrant, radiant, healthy, balanced, *unlimited* Being that You Are?

If so, then make a clear choice to *remember and know* the Truth of Who You Are.

Make a clear choice to *become aware.* Know that once you make a clear choice, the universe responds immediately.

You can even ask for assistance from the non-physical realms.

Your *cognitive mind* has been programmed by the duality of the Third Dimension; it has been programmed into limitation and into believing that you're somehow not good enough. Your cognitive mind will always lead you into limitation and 'not enough'...that's its job. (Remember: we came here specifically to explore limitation.) Besides...if you could 'figure out' your life... wouldn't you have already done it?

If you are now ready to 'remove the veil' and move beyond limitation into the fullness of Your Being, then you'll have to stop relying on your cognitive mind and begin to start following the *knowing* in your *HEART.*

Knowing is natural. Knowing just IS. You just *know.*

Learn to *discern* and trust your *knowing* (vs. your *thinking*). Have you ever gone ahead and done something even though you *had a bad feeling* about it? How did it turn out? Not so good, right? Why? Because you went against your *knowing*. That 'bad feeling' was your *knowing* telling you that the tightness you felt inside was your signal that you were heading in a direction that would ultimately work against you. Conversely, have you ever been presented with an opportunity that made your heart sing and your eyes light up? How did that turn out? A little better than the previous scenario, I presume? Why? Because you trusted your knowing! Your inner guidance was the *feeling* of joy and possibility. It felt expansive and happy. These are signals that you are going in a direction that will have a positive outcome.

Your inner knowing is communicated through *feeling...**not*** through *thinking!* The heart feels and the mind thinks. The feelings in the heart carry the Inner Wisdom. Trying to rationalize and think yourself into health *does not work...*have you noticed? Learn to discern between the things that feel restrictive and give you *a bad feeling,* and the options that feel open, light and 'good.' Learn how to *feel* what you *know.*

*It's time to stop thinking and rationalizing and start **knowing!***

Your inner knowing will never lead you astray. It will lead you straight back to the grandness of *YOU!*

Take the Fear Out

It is absolutely essential that you release the fear. Fear is the Grand Inhibitor. Fear and worry block knowingness. Fear is False Evidence Appearing Real. Fear and worry are simply projecting something unwanted into your future. By worrying about what we fear, we actually create exactly what we *don't* want because that is where our attention is focused.

If you're looking at your current situation with fear, worry and dread, that's okay. Your reaction is normal, but it is not helpful. Let's see if we can re-frame your perspective, take the fear out and return you to your true inner knowing.

Fear is created from the outside world. This reality teaches us that we are *unsafe* and that we must protect ourselves...whether it be with helmets, with seat belts, with guns or with pharmaceuticals.

This reality teaches that we can't trust strangers, that we have to trust the 'experts' and that we definitely can't trust ourselves. This reality is limiting and confusing and it causes us to doubt ourselves. When we're in doubt, we're not operating from our knowingness. When we're not operating from our knowingness, we're prone to fear.

Your Inner Being is an infinitely brilliant and capable healer. Your Inner Being has no fear. The part of you that is experiencing the fear is the 'little human' aspect of You. Let's reconnect you to your Inner Being so you can see the fear for what it is, and release it...then you'll be infinitely better equipped to re-create your current circumstances.

If you're experiencing fear of a disease, remember that the 'disease' (the name by which doctors refer to your condition) is just a name that has been given by the medical community to a grouping of similar symptoms. Your body is displaying these symptoms because you were unaware that it was communicating to you in more subtle ways prior to this. When your body was displaying subtle *dis*-ease, you didn't receive the message. Your body kept communicating, but you kept missing the message. Now, your body has *finally* caught your attention!

This is good news, because now that you're paying attention, you can address the energetic cause of the imbalance and allow your body to rebalance itself. Fortunately, the capacity for rebalancing is built right into your body! If you learn to work together with it, your body will automatically rebalance itself.

Your body knows how to rebalance itself and bring itself back into health, but it needs for you to get out of its way! It needs for you to **not** be in fear and resistance. It needs for you to *know* and *trust* that your body knows what to do. It needs for you to trust it... by trusting *Yourself*. It needs for you to love it! *Yes!* If your body was your lover, would it still be with you? Would you be willing to fall back in love...with your body?

So I'll ask again...if you treated your lover the way that you treat your body, would you still be together? Think about it! Don't you appreciate it when your loved ones show you kindness, consideration and respect? When they say *please* and *thank you*, *I love you*, and *I appreciate you?* Do you treat others better than you treat your own body? Do you show your body respect and consideration, or do you ignore it? Do you allow it to move the way it wants to? Do you feed it what it actually requires, rather than what *you think* it needs? If you now see that you've not been treating your body very well, is it any wonder that it is unbalanced?

It is highly likely that your body has been crying out for your attention! Showing your body some tender care and loving attention will go a very long way in dispelling the fear and will greatly enhance the healing process!

Your body is *not* trying to sabotage you! There is absolutely no reason to fear or resent your body! Your body *loves* you! Your body *desires* to be healthy and fit and live a very long life! Are you willing to start *partnering with* your body instead of rejecting it, resenting it and neglecting it?

Would you be willing to let your Inner Being...the non-physical part of You that is always in balance and well-Being...start to take the lead? Would you allow your cognitive mind to step aside and let your Inner Being and your body bring you and your life back into balance? Would you be willing to know YourSelf as infinite and unlimited? Would you be willing to make 'infinite well-Being' the platform for your reality and recognize that anything contrary to that is a distortion? Would yo be willing to realize that there is absolutely *nothing* for You...the Infinite, Unlimited Being... to fear?

Take the Name Off It

Let's look at a very simple insight I had that changed everything for me when it comes to my body and its ability to rebalance itself:

One day, after being on my spiritual path for quite a long time, I 'caught a cold.' I awoke in the morning with a sore throat, stuffy nose and a pressure behind my eyes. My mind immediately thought, 'oh, great...here we go...' and it immediately began to plan the logical progression of my *cold:* sore throat, runny nose and stuffy head: duration 2–3 days. Sore throat subsides, congestion moves into chest and coughing begins: 3–4 more days, symptoms slowly subside and linger: up to another week. Ugh!

Then it hit me: *what if I don't make this into 'a cold'? What if I allow this to simply be my body clearing itself?*

I had already begun to notice that colds, the flu, rashes, diarrhea, sudden bouts of being tired...are all completely natural and normal ways for the body to clear, cleanse, and re-balance itself. These symptoms, in and of themselves, do not automatically mean that you are 'sick.' Sometimes these symptoms are the quickest and easiest ways for the body to rebalance itself.

I knew that if I bought into my symptoms as *a cold*, that it would have to act like *a cold*. However, I knew that on some level it was just my body clearing itself. So I immediately took the *Cold* label off my symptoms and replaced it with: *my body's just clearing itself*. I did this by feeling into the energies of *a cold*, then feeling into the energies of *body clearing itself*. I noticed that the two energies felt different. I noticed that 'body clearing itself' felt lighter (more true) than 'cold.' I then made a clear choice as to which option was my truth. I then asked my body to clear itself quickly and easily and within 24 hours the cycle was complete and the symptoms were gone. I've never had *a cold* since then, and the once or twice that my body has had to clear itself with scratchy throat or runny nose, it has only been for a few short hours.

Now, this was not about the word 'cold'...it was about awareness. It was about the awareness of what energetic constructs are involved in *having a cold*, and the awareness of the energetics of *body clearing itself*. It was about placing my *awareness* on the difference between *having a cold* and the natural process of *body clearing itself*, then *discerning* what was my true knowing. I had to become aware of the difference between the *programming of this reality* vs. my *inner knowing*.

This was a very important lesson for me...to *take the label off!*

I realize that this sounds simplistic, but it is actually really significant. This was *huge* in my ability to allow my body to rebalance itself from my experience of cancer that I had created.

This reality teaches us that each physical 'condition,' whether it is a common cold or cancer, has its own set of characteristics... its own course...a progression...a pattern of how the symptoms are supposed to play out in physical reality. What if it doesn't have to be like that?

If you say that you *have cancer* (or a *cold*, or *arthritis*, or any other condition), then it has to be manifest as that in your reality and you must follow the 'rules' of that condition. That is the way that consciousness works. We are constantly creating our reality, so if you *have cancer* then that is what *has* to show up in your reality... that's just the way the universe works. If you want to change your condition, then *change your condition!*...Take the name off it! Allow it to become *my body has temporarily gotten out of balance* or *my body is re-balancing itself.*

Think of it this way: would you rather *have (cancer, arthritis, diabetes, etc.)* or would you prefer: *my body is temporarily out of balance?*

If your body is out of balance, it's really not a horrible thing, because your body *knows* how to rebalance itself! If you get yourself out of its way, by becoming aware and communicating with it, your body *absolutely can* rebalance itself! However, if you *have cancer,* or *have arthritis,* etc., then you also have to *have* all of the symptoms, conditions, timelines, progressions and prognoses that are connected to that condition. That's how it works. You can't *have* the condition and *not have* it...that is impossible.

Right here, you might be saying...*I've already been diagnosed! I have (xyz). It's here..it's real! I can't deny that!*

I'm not saying to deny or ignore it...that is just resistance...nor am I trying to trivialize your experience. However, if you wish to rid yourself of the condition, then you have to *stop 'having'* it!

You can't **have** *(xyz) and also* **not have** *it....*it's as simple as that. Which do you choose? Would you be willing to *stop 'having'* the condition so that you can return your body to health?

You may wish to re-read this section a few times until you can feel into the larger truths behind the words. What else do you know about this that you haven't been aware of as yet?

Trust the Expert

We're taught by this reality that we should trust the experts. Whether it is doctors, lawyers, accountants, or mechanics...we're taught that we don't know as much as other people. We're taught that we don't know enough, and that we should trust those who have more experience.

Now, there are many experts in many fields, and many who are truly excellent at what they do. It certainly makes good sense and saves a lot of time and aggravation to have a skilled mechanic work on your car when you know very little about the inner workings of an engine, or to have a certified accountant handle your taxes when you have little knowledge of the intricacies of the tax laws. When it comes to doctors, there are many physicians and surgeons who are highly skilled and who truly have their patients best interest at heart. This section is in no way meant to demean or diminish doctors in any way. But let's take a look at what a doctor's true role is.

Do you know that it is *NOT* the doctor's job to heal you? *Wait,..What?!?*

It is *not* the doctor's job to heal you...it is *YOUR* job to heal You! The doctor (or healer, energy practitioner, medicine man, or witch doctor) can not *create the healing for you!* There is *no one else* who can heal you. The only one who can heal you is YOU!

The true role of any doctor or healer is to create a safe space and use their abilities, skills and knowledge to help facilitate *your* healing **process.They** are offering conditions by which the healing energies of Source (which *you* have summoned), can flow to and through them...to you. You and your healer are in an agreement to work together to rebalance your body, but it is *You* who must take the lead. They are there to support and assist *You*. Making *them* responsible for *your* health is not fair to them and it is not taking responsibility for yourself.

No matter how many credentials, diplomas, awards, or medals the healer has accrued, no matter their level of expertise in the fields of medicine and healing, it is *not* their job to create the healing *for* you, and when it comes to *your* body, there is only ONE expert in the entire Universe...and that expert is YOU! There is no other being in all of creation who knows your body better than you do. Doctors and healers have great insight and expertise; they are very skilled at what they do, and they have a vested interest in your health, but when it comes to *creating YOUR* health...that is up to You! No one else can create health *for* you! You are the one and only creator of your life.

This is why it is imperative that you learn to listen to your body and start trusting your inner knowing.

Most people choose to consult physicians. This can be helpful, or, if you've given your power over to the physician, expecting them to *do it for you*, it can prove to be challenging. Physicians are wonderful people who wish to help you, but they are not trained to be intuitive. They are trained by *the system,* which trains them to diagnose the symptoms they see into categories (arthritis, cancer, kidney disease, etc.) and to prescribe corresponding pharmaceuticals. Can pharmaceuticals be helpful? Of course! Are they what your body actually requires to rebalance itself? Maybe... maybe not. That is for *you and your body* to discern in the moment. *Interesting side note:* Have you ever noticed that physicians usually prescribe *pharmaceutical* 'remedies' as opposed to herbs, supplements, essential oils or other *natural* remedies? Might it be beneficial to be able to discern what your body *truly* requires rather than blindly following 'doctor's orders'?

Getting a diagnosis from a physician can be highly beneficial. If you're exhibiting symptoms of imbalance, it can be very helpful to know what has manifest in your body, so you can more accurately address it. Perhaps there is a very simple remedy that can be prescribed, and along with addressing the energetic cause you can easily bring your body back into full balance very quickly.

Do you need to get a diagnosis from a doctor? What does your *knowing* tell you? What does your body require? Does it need outside assistance, or can you and your body work together to re-balance? Does your body require medication? Does it require herbs? How about energy work or acupuncture? Perhaps the healing powers of essential oils or flower essences might be what your body needs? Use your skills with muscle testing and discern what your body actually requires.

When the body goes into discomfort, the mind usually kicks into the *danger!* zone. Your mind was designed to process input from this physical reality, and its main job is to protect the body. It's going to use all of its *logic* to try to protect you. However, *logic* and *knowing* are two very different things. If your logical mind really protected you, would you be in this current predicament? I don't think so!

Don't trust your logical mind...trust your *knowing.*

Your logical mind will try to rationalize your situation and come up with a logical solution. But remember: your mind is operating from within the 'box' of the Third Dimension...the box we are now stepping out of! Logic is designed to keep you 'in the box.' It is designed to keep you limited. Remember: that's how the game of this reality is played. 'Logic' is designed to keep you from your *knowing*. However, you have the ability to tune into your knowing. Your *knowing* will never betray you. Your *inner knowing* is your direct connection to your Soul. Your Soul will never lead you astray.

It is also very important to be aware that your doctor has been trained by *the system*, and you want to be aware of how *the system* is set up: it is controlled by the pharmaceutical companies and the insurance industry. This is neither *good* nor *bad,* but it is something that is worth *being aware* of. How is your physician being influenced in his diagnoses and prescriptions? Your physician was trained to look for *what's wrong* and what *pills* or *procedures* can *fix* it and what procedures the insurance companies will approve. This is the 'box' of this limited reality...the game. Do you wish to continue to play in the *limitation game* as if it was real, or are you ready to step outside the box of this reality and allow your body to rebalance itself by returning to the *un*limited Being You Are? Your physician can be of great assistance to you, but YOU must be discerning. YOU must take the lead! YOU must take full responsibility for your own body!

YOU are the expert when it comes to your body. You can heal your body by yourSelf or with the help of others. You can take medications, herbs, supplements or you can use certain foods. There is no *one right way* to rebalance your body. It is a completely unique process for each one of us. Which path is best for *You?*

Choose

If your body is in a state of imbalance, let me ask you a question: why are you slowly killing yourself?

What?!?

Yes...think about it: your *natural state of Being* is vibrant, radiant health. The only one who can interrupt that flow is You. You interrupt the flow by resisting. So what are you resisting? What are you *dying* to avoid? Why are you not allowing yourself to fully, freely participate in life? What are you afraid of? Why are you allowing your body to slowly break down until it quits?

Would you be willing to *choose LIFE?*

No matter what your life looks like in this moment, *You* have the power to change it! You can create *anything* you choose! You are a Creator. That is your True Nature. You can't *not be* a Creator. You can shut off your awareness, but you are still creating in every moment...consciously or unconsciously. Up until now, for the most part, you've been creating *unconsciously.* Would you be willing to try *consciously creating,* for a change?

Health is a choice.

What?!

Yes...health is a choice. We are trained by this reality to believe that we are victims, that we are susceptible to disease and that we are 'lucky' if we are healthy. Nothing could be further from the truth. (Remember...this 'land of limitation' is designed to allow us to explore ourselves as the *opposite* of who we really are.)

Do you remember the exercise from earlier in the book about *finding playful and happy?* Happiness is a choice. You can *choose* to be happy. You can also *choose* to be healthy!

Would you be willing to *choose* to be healthy? How about wealthy? That's also a choice!

How do you choose that?

You choose it by CHOOSING it. You make a Soul-Level choice. You say, "I Am That I AM...I EXIST, therefore I CHOOSE."..and you FEEL the choice in the core of your Being. You also *know* that your choice is available. You are an Infinite Being...You can choose *anything*...because *everything* is available. Once you choose health, then place that choice right in the center of Your Being and focus your attention on it. KNOW that *healthy* is where you're now heading and don't settle for less. Don't allow yourself to get stuck by focusing on discomfort. Recognize the discomfort and take any actions that your body requires, but stay focused on the health you are choosing. Know that *radiant health* is the greater truth of your Being.

Once you make a *real, true CHOICE*...something amazing happens: the Universe rearranges itself to reflect your choice! That's how it works. Remember: you are creating your own reality. As you create, the Universe reflects your creation back to you... that's how the Universe works. But you have to really *choose*...mere lip service won't work! Simply saying "yeah, I choose health" and then continuing on in the same old patterns of unbalance will *not* create health.

You must *choose* and then *act* accordingly. You must become consciously *aware* of what you are choosing, and then act *in accordance* with your choice.

What does that mean? That means that if you make a *true choice* for health, then you have *know* that the Universe immediately begins to respond and you have to *know* that your body knows how to rebalance itself, and then you have to honor your body's needs by communicating with it, listening to it and following through with whatever actions are required.

Knowing vs. Believing

Just because I have told you how the Universe works and that you can choose health, *don't believe me!*

What?!?

You heard me...don't *believe* anything anyone tells you!

Why? Because *believing* is simply the flip side of the *'not knowing'* coin!

What?

Okay...here's a question for you: do you *believe* that you can breathe, or do you simply *know* that you can breathe? Do you need to *believe* that you can breathe in order to breathe, or do you just breathe?

It's very important to distinguish between what you *believe* and what you *know*. Believing is just another way of *not* knowing.

*You can't create what you desire by **believing** that you can create it...you must **know** that you can create it.*

How do you **know?** By practicing. By becoming aware. By tuning in to your Inner Being.

Do you *believe* that you are a kind person...or are you kind? Do you *believe* that you are generous... or are you generous? Are you beginning to see the distinction here?

What do you *know* to be true about you? Are you funny? Do you like to laugh? What is your best quality? What do you love most about yourSelf? What do you enjoy most about this planet? Where is your favorite place on this planet? What do you *know* about yourSelf that no one else on this planet knows? What do you *know* about your true greatness? What do you know about your greatness that you have kept hidden from the rest of the world... and maybe even from yourself?

As you answer these questions, can you *feel* your *knowing?* Can you sense the difference between knowing and believing? Do you have to *believe* that you are kind in order to BE kind?

Start discerning the difference between what you *believe* and what you *know* and watch your life change in ways that you couldn't have imagined!

What beliefs are you holding onto that are actually *blocking* your true knowing? Do you believe that you can't change your physical condition because someone once told you that it was unchangeable? Is that actually true? Is anything in this reality actually *unchangeable?* What does your *inner knowing* tell you?

What beliefs can you let go of, that if you let go of them, would allow you to *know* yourSelf into a life beyond your wildest dreams?

Oh, and by the way...

Saying *I don't know*...is simply a way of **choosing to be unaware.**

Say what?!

Yes. Because the truth is...You **do** know. You are intricately connected to *You*...to *All That You Are*...and to the *field of awareness* of the All That Is. You know everything there is to know about *You*, and you have access to all the knowledge of the entire Universe. Anything you *choose* to know, you *can* know. Saying *I don't know* is a lie. Because the truth is...You *do* know! The truth is that You Are a Grand, Empowered, Infinite Being of Magnitude! Why are you believing that you are small and powerless? Would you be willing to release those lies that you've been be*lie*ving are truths?

Are you willing to delete *I don't know* from your vocabulary and start standing in the power of your *knowing?*

Feeling Vibrant, Radiant Health

If your body is out of balance and you're not experiencing yourself as healthy, it is going to be very important to make a clear choice as to how you would prefer to experience your health. What state of health and vitality would you like to experience?

For me, I chose *vibrant, radiant health*...so let's explore that choice.

Once you make the choice for vibrant, radiant health, you must practice *feeling* vibrant, radiant health! By feeling it, you are consciously bringing yourself into *vibrational alignment* with the *frequency* of vibrant, radiant health. As you tune into vibrant, radiant health, it will feel *good*. Why? Because it is your Truth. It is Who You Are. Whenever you are BEing the True You...it will feel good!

If you've been in the *habit* of feeling unwell, you will need to develop a new habit...the habit of feeling healthy. And, yes, I did use the word *habit*. You have developed the habit of focusing on *what's wrong with me*...and your body's been responding by creating something to be wrong with you...*Thank you, dear amazing, wonderful body!...I AM now choosing something different! I choose to remember Who I Really Am...the radiantly healthy Me!*

You must now develop a new, *empowering* habit. You must re-train yourself to develop a new point of focus. Spend some time each day focusing on the FEELING of vibrant, radiant health. Imagine it! Imagine what it feels like, imagine what activities you will enjoy with your healthy, strong body. Breathe with that healthy body and begin letting your body know that this is the direction you're choosing.

As you *feel* into it...is there a certain *color* that would represent your radiantly healthy body? Clear your mind, feel into *radiant health* and allow a color to appear. Don't go looking for it...just allow it to come into your awareness. What color represents your body as it currently is? Is that color different? Imagine your whole body in its current color, then allow the color of *radiant health* to flow into your body, and watch as the new color transmutes the current color. Allow for the colors to change each time you do this little exercise...this is another instance of 'you can't do it wrong'! Trust the images you perceive! Allow the colors of radiant health to permeate every single cell of your entire body.

Bathe your cells in love...in light...breathe life into every cell of your body and let your body radiate its health out into the world!

Imagine what foods your healthy, strong body will require. Does it eat the same things you are currently consuming? Does it need extra water? Does your current body need some extra nutrients to help it rebalance? Remember to *ask your body what it requires.* Use muscle testing to determine what and how much your body wants and needs.

What changes can you implement today to begin to bring yourself into *vibrational alignment* with your *radiantly healthy* body?

Know and Trust

Knowing and *trusting* go hand-in-hand. But in this reality, we have gotten our *knowing* and our *trusting* very distorted.

Knowing is just that: *knowing.* If you know something, then there is no need for belief systems around it, and no need to defend that knowing. For example: do you *know* that you can breathe? Is there any need to *believe* that you can breathe? If someone questioned your ability to breathe, would you feel a need to get angry and defensive and try to prove to them that they are wrong? Or would you simply take a deep breath and chuckle at their silliness?

Have you ever done something that no one else thought you could do, but you went ahead and did it anyway because you already *knew* you could? Feel into that for a moment...notice how there's no doubt, no second-guessing, no need to believe...just pure *knowing.* You had complete *TRUST in yourself.*

In this day and age, our abilities to trust ourselves has been greatly diminished. We're taught to *trust the experts* because *they* know better than *we* do. How many *experts* in the financial world have turned out to be expert *embezzlers*? How many people chose to *blindly trust* those 'experts' and then lost all their money?

We're trained to put our trust in doctors for our health. Now, this is not to say that doctors are bad! Not at all! This is to say that we have, to a great extent, stopped taking responsibility for our own health and given that responsibility over to our doctors. We have to go for a check up to find out if we are healthy or not! If we are ill, we have the doctors *tell us what to do.* We no longer have an intimate dialog with our own bodies! Our bodies are constantly communicating to us, but instead of listening to them, we go to *someone else* to tell us what *they think* about *our* body!

Does that even make sense?

Is it *fair* to the doctors to make *them* responsible for *our* health?

82

Can someone else heal you? *No!* You are the only one who can bring yourself back into balance. It is *your* choice...*your* responsibility. Others can assist you and support you, but don't trust *someone else* to *do it for you*...it disempowers you and it is not fair to them!

Doctors and healers are wonderful people! They do what they do because they have a sincere interest in promoting health and well-being. They can be excellent partners to help you return to balance, but they cannot *do it for you.*

It is time for you to stop *blindly trusting* 'the experts' without checking in with your own inner wisdom! How many of the people who lost all their money to an embezzler had a *bad feeling* somewhere along the line that they ignored because *'well...he's the expert...what do I know?'* In hind sight, they knew *a lot*, but they had shut off their awareness and given their power over to someone else.

Just because a doctor prescribes something for you, doesn't necessarily mean that it is really what your body needs! Remember: you are unique...one of a kind...an *individual* unlike any other Being in all of creation! Your needs are *yours* alone! Just because 80 million other people take 'xyz' doesn't mean that is right for you... *it might be,* but check in with your body! What does your *inner knowing* tell you? Stop blindly following other people's advice! No one in the entirety of all Creation knows more about You than YOU!

Stop *blindly trusting* the 'experts' and *start trusting YourSelf!*
Start *trusting YOUR knowing!*

By opening up your awareness and developing absolute *trust* in your own *inner knowing,* no one will be able to steer you wrong ever again!

What would your life be like if you *trusted yourself* implicitly?

What if you could just *know* how to bring your body back into balance?

What if you could make a clear choice for health and balance and then have complete *trust*...absolute *knowing*...that the universe (called *You*) will guide you directly to your desired outcome?

Are you willing to trust your inner knowing?

SECTION FIVE:
Effective Tools

This section is filled with practical tools that can be used together or independently on a daily basis to ground, center and balance yourself and your energetic field. These tools are simple, highly effective ways to create an environment of personal empowerment and well-being. When used consistently, these tools will allow you to become balanced and centered, which will greatly enhance your mental clarity, intuition and knowingness.

They are designed to bring you back into a space of well-being.

You cannot be aligned with well-being from within the space of imbalance. You must focus your attention on the space of well-being in order to align with it. For example: if you have fallen into a pit of quicksand, if the only thing you are focused on is the quicksand itself, you will rapidly sink. In order to extricate yourself, you'll need to turn your attention away from *where you are* and focus on where you'd *rather be*. This is what Albert Einstein meant when he said that you can't solve a problem on the same level it was created.

In order to return to health from a space of imbalance, you must turn your focus away from where you are, to where you'd rather be. You're not trying to ignore or deny the quicksand, but you *must* move your attention away from *it*, and train your focus on your desired destination.

Once you expand your focus beyond the quicksand, you'll be able to notice possible solutions. This reality is very much like the quicksand. We've been floundering, focusing only on the quicksand...this is the *limited human* aspect of ourselves. Once we move our focus away from the quicksand and turn our focus onto our surroundings (the larger, non-physical aspect of ourselves) then assistance can be obtained from any number of possible sources...even sources that we might not be able to immediately see and had no idea were there.

Are you ready to get out of the quicksand?

These tools will help you to turn your focus away from the quicksand and onto your desired destination.

Tool 1. Breathe

Yes...simple, *conscious, intentional* breathing. It sounds much too simple to be effective, right?

Wrong!

Of course, we breathe all the time...we don't even have to think about it. But, when was the last time you actually focused on a breath? Go ahead...give it a try! Take a nice, big breath and feel it draw into your lungs. Feel your lungs expand. Then watch as the breath leaves on the exhale. Watch it again...can you see the breath come in? Can you watch as it fill your lungs? Can you watch it leave on the exhale?

Did you just notice something weird? Did you just notice how you could actually *watch* the breath?

Wow! How cool is that?! How can that be?

Congratulations!...You just opened up to the inter-dimensional, non-physical aspect of You! Wow!

You mean...there is a part of Me that sees without using my eyes?

Yup... you got it! Pretty neat, huh? *Hmmm...* I wonder what else you can see without using your eyes? Okay...back to the breath.

There are thousands upon thousands of different breathing techniques. This is not about any *technique*. This is about *awareness*.

Conscious breathing is about expanding your awareness. The breath is the point of connection between *you*, the limited human, and *You*, the Infinite Being...the multi-dimensional, non-physical part of You that is able to *watch* the breath. Picture planet Earth...

now picture yourself sitting on the planet...now picture the Infinite, non-physical You totally surrounding the planet. The breath is what connects you to You. It allows you (the human aspect) to expand beyond the confines of physicality and into the realms of the Infinite You.

The breath is how the Infinite You can send you information. Imagine with each breath that your Soul is sending you love. Do you have a physical issue? Ask your Soul for assistance and then breathe into that area. Watch as the breath comes down through the top of your head (your crown chakra) and watch as it moves into the area of concern in your body. Watch the breath light up that area. Feel the love that your Soul is sending to you within each breath. Watch that area as the light and love from your Soul penetrates and soothes the area, bringing balance, ease and harmony. Watch as your body and your Soul begin to breathe in harmony.

Breathe and *connect* to your Soul.

Breathe and *connect* to the well-being that is *YOURS*...it already belongs to you! It is Who You *Are!*

Breathe and *connect* to the love your Soul has for you.

Breathe and *connect* to the radiance and vitality that are already *yours.*

Breathe with awareness. Breathe with ease. You can *not* do it wrong...it is impossible, so just relax and breathe with focused attention!

Ask your Soul for assistance...then breathe it in. Ask to be shown balance or ease.

...or ask your Body to show you what radiant health feels like.

...or ask your Soul to guide you back to well-being.

...or ask your Body what it requires.

Then sit and breathe...*without any expectation*...and simply notice what you notice.

If you'd like a really simple breathing exercise, here's one of my favorites:

Quiet your mind and bring your awareness to your breath. Then, gently become aware of the center of the Earth. Imagine a tube that runs down through your body to the center of the Earth. Now imagine that tube stretching all the way up to the Great Central Sun. As you focus on the Great Central Sun, inhale the light from the Sun down through the tube into your heart. From your heart space, exhale the light down into the Earth Star at the core of the Earth. Then, inhale the light back up into your heart space, and exhale it up and out through the top of your head to the Great Central Sun. As you repeat this pattern, you'll most likely find yourself feeling greatly relaxed and centered within just a few short, focused breaths.

Conscious breathing doesn't have to be complicated. It doesn't have to take a long time. You can't do it *wrong*...and there are no *right* ways, either! How about that? You can't fail!

How about this idea....take just *ONE,* deep conscious breath... and *say hello to your body*...fill your body with ease, with balance, with vitality...draw it down from your Soul...fill your body with the love that You Are. *Feel* and *watch* the breath as it comes in through the top of your head and moves down through your body all the way to the tips of your toes.

How might your body respond if you *consciously* breathe into it and acknowledge it each day? I wonder if your body would begin to respond differently? Would you be willing to give conscious breathing a try?

Tool 2. Ground

Grounding is a very useful tool for us to use on a daily basis. Grounding means to energetically connect yourself to the Earth.

There are many methods for grounding yourself, but the simplest and easiest way to describe it that I know of is to 'grow roots' out of the soles of your feet. Allow those roots to grow down into the earth, passing all the way down to the core the Earth. Allow your roots to wrap around the core of the Earth. Feel the connection that has been created between you and Mother Earth. Breathe and feel. This does not have to be complicated.

This exercise, is extremely simple, yet highly effective. Your mind may want to tell you that this is silly because you're just 'making it up,' but rest assured, you are *consciously creating* a very *real* connection to the Earth! Simply because a creation is non-physical does not mean it is not real!

So, why do we need to do this?

Well, grounding helps keep us present and balanced in our bodies. As humans, we tend to wander off into the mental realms very easily, allowing us to not be present in our bodies. Do you know people who are flighty, absent-minded, accident-prone or scattered? These are all symptoms of not being grounded in the body.

Grounding also helps to siphon off stray electrical charges from the energy field around us. We have electro-magnetic fields surrounding our bodies. As we interact with the world around us, we are constantly bombarded by the energies in the atmosphere. By keeping ourselves grounded, we become less likely to become adversely affected by the energies around us as the 'static charges' are removed from our energy fields.

Also, the Earth has a very stabilizing effect on our energy fields. By keeping ourselves connected to the Earth, we share our energies with the Earth and we are then able to benefit from the calm, balanced, soothing, stabilizing energies that Mother Earth can offer us.

If you are new to grounding, take notice of your current state of energy. Take a few minutes to ground yourself, and then take notice of your energy once again. Do you notice a difference? Are you more relaxed? More calm? Do you have more space? Notice what you notice. Make a commitment to yourself to remember to ground daily, and see what effect it has.

Tool 3. Ask: Where Is This Coming From?

Just because you are *experiencing* something doesn't necessarily mean that it is *yours!*

Say what?! What are you talking about?

Yes! Check this out: our bodies are surrounded by an electromagnetic field. This electromagnetic field acts like an antenna...a radio receiver. It is constantly picking up signals (vibrational frequencies) from all around it. The signals could be coming from any number of sources including: mass consciousness, friends, family members, solar flares or the Earth herself.

When your electromagnetic field is in perfect alignment...in perfect harmony and balance, the signals just pass through your field without adversely affecting you. However, when there are energetic *distortions* in your field, the signals 'bounce' off the distortions, the distortions *activate* and cause a feeling of un-ease.

What is a distortion?

A *distortion* is a belief pattern that has gotten embedded in your field that is out of alignment with the truth of who you are. It is any kind of belief that states: *I'm not good enough, I don't fit in, I'm not smart enough* or any other variation of *there's something wrong with me.* Because the real truth is: there is NOTHING 'wrong' with you! You are a Divine Being *made of the perfection* of The All That Is.

For a visual, you can think of a wide open, gently flowing river. (This is You.) Now, visualize big boulders scattered throughout the course of the riverbed (these are the distortions). Can you see how the water bumps up against the rocks, pushes against them and has to flow around them? The boulders disrupt the smooth, harmonious flow of the river. The boulders cause *resistance* to the flow.

How do my beliefs become 'boulders'?

Well, the field surrounding your body is electromagnetic. Thoughts are electrical and emotions are magnetic. When a distorted belief is coupled with a strong emotion, the combination forms a 'clump' in your field. So let's say you've got a belief that says, "I don't fit in," so when you find yourself in social situations, you feel a level of anxiety. So now you have 'anxiety' as a 'rock' in your field.

Now that *anxiety* is hanging out in your energetic field (held in place by *I don't fit in*), it will now become activated by frequencies of similar vibration (like attracts like). These frequencies could come from a wide range of sources: anything from solar flares to coming in near range of someone else who is currently feeling anxious.

Have you ever started to feel anxious for no apparent reason? What happened as soon as you felt 'anxious'...your mind started to look for the *reason,* right? (*What's wrong with me* that I am feeling anxious?) And it didn't take long for it to come up with one, did it? As soon as your mind finds a *reason* and *grabs onto it,* the anxiety suddenly 'becomes' yours.

Can you see how that anxiety was triggered by something *external* to you, but you easily *internalized* it and made it your own?

Do you know that almost ALL of your thoughts and emotions *ARE NOT YOURS?* You are picking them up from your surrounding environment!

Seriously?

Yes!

So when your body feels something...anything...even aches or pains...(yes! those too!)...realize that it might simply be your body picking up signals from the surrounding environment.

When you notice that you're feeling an undesirable emotion or an ache or pain, begin to ask *where is this coming from?* Once you've become adept at listening to your body and your inner knowing, the answer to this question *most* of the time will be a realization that...*Wow! It's not mine!*

As soon as you realize that it isn't yours, thank your body for the message and let it know that there is nothing more your body needs to do with the information. It can just release it.

Here's a real-life example of this: I once walked into a place and sat down next to a friend. Within minutes of sitting down, my neck suddenly began to spasm. I didn't know why. After a few minutes, my friend turned to me and said, "Man! My neck has been so sore today!" *Bingo!* I had picked up on someone else's 'stuff'! It wasn't *my* neck pain! As soon as I realized it wasn't mine, I laughed, took some beep breaths into my neck and let my body know that it wasn't *my* pain and that it didn't need to alert me of the pain signals it was picking up on. The pain released immediately.

How much of the imbalance in your body is actually *not* yours, but you've been inadvertently carrying it around, thinking that it *was* yours, because *you* were feeling it?

Are you a healer or caregiver by nature? Have you inadvertently been trying to help others heal themselves by taking on their pain for them? Have you ever seen a friend or family member suffer and wished that you could ease their pain? Would you be willing to take on the pain to help ease their suffering? If so, you're at risk of doing exactly that. **But, be aware!** You can **not** heal someone else's issues! Their pain is theirs alone! Making *yourself* sick can NOT help them...it is impossible!

Is it possible that your imbalance is actually *not* yours?

I'll even go one step farther...and get ready...because this might really make you upset! If it does...*good!* (It is a great opportunity for you to see if you are arguing to keep your limitations!) If you get upset, be sure to ask yourself *what does my inner knowing know about this?* And be sure to ask yourself if this is the reality you really wish to create.

Are you ready? Here it is:

Your physical imbalance is NOT yours!

WHAT?! That's crazy talk!

Nope! Check this out: no matter what your 'condition', whether it is 'premature gray hair', baldness, arthritis, cancer...you name it...it existed somewhere in the hologram before you 'contracted' it. Therefore, it already existed in someone else's (or many other people's) reality, right?

Well...yeah...and your point is?

My point is...you've 'contracted' someone else's reality!

HOLY COW! Seriously?

Yep. You've picked up on a pre-existing condition and brought it into your awareness, *bought into it* as a viable possibility, held it locked into your consciousness as a belief system, your body reflected that belief back to you, and then when it manifest, *you simply assumed that it was yours!*

But it's mine now! I'm the one suffering with it!

So...here's a HUGE opportunity for you! Would you like to CHOOSE something different? Here are your choices as I see them: (What choices do *YOU* see?)

You can choose that your condition is YOURS. If you choose that it is *yours*, then you're choosing to make it solid and real. You're choosing that the condition is real, that it is an entity unto itself and that you *have it*. Truth: is this the choice you truly desire, or is this the choice that you believe is your only option? If you think it is your only option...then you may wish to read this book a few more times! ...Let's explore another option right now:

You can choose that your condition is NOT yours. That's right! You can choose that *right now*...no questions asked! If you choose that it's *not yours*, then *it doesn't belong to you! Release it!* If it doesn't belong to you, might it be a little easier to let it go? Do you have to keep something that you don't want that doesn't even belong to you in the first place? *No!*

But that's waaaay to simplistic! You can't just go POOF! and release a physical condition...

Okay...fair point.

But does your mind think that something that simple couldn't possibly work because there obviously have to be many other components involved? And because there are obviously so many other steps involved, *'It's not mine...I release it'* is pointless?

Is it true that something that *simple* couldn't possibly work? Let's look at this using an analogy:

Let's say that you're in New York City and you get a sudden urge to drive to Los Angeles. Is it possible that you could just hop in the car and drive across the country from NY to LA? Yes? Well, that's pretty darn simple, isn't it?

But then again...it's not *exactly* that simple, is it? You'd have to spend weeks planning. You'd have to make the time in your schedule. You'd have to get directions. You'd have to have gas in the car. You'd have to be sure the car is in working order. You'll probably want to pack some extra clothes and maybe some water and snacks for the trip. You'll have to figure out which route to take. What if you make a wrong turn and start heading in the wrong direction? What about paying tolls? Will you drive straight through or will you have to find hotels along the way? Do you have a map or a GPS? Will someone go with you or do you wish to travel solo? Do you want to visit family or friends on the way?

Wow...this is getting more complicated by the minute!

Exactly! Do you see that, if you think that you have to know all the details in advance, you might become overwhelmed and not even bother to take the trip?

Do you see where I'm going with this? Can you just *hop in the car and drive* to LA, or does it have to be a huge, complicated deal...having to *figure out* 'how' the trip will unfold in advance? If you hop in the car and start driving, won't all of the details (gas, food, lodging, etc.) *naturally* take care of themselves along the way?

What if you could choose that the physical imbalance is *not* yours and simply release it?

What if that *simple, clear choice* would *automatically* draw to you all of the necessary components?

Which trip would you rather take...the *hop in the car and drive* or the multi-detailed, complicated one that must be figured out in advance?

Which 'condition' will be easier to release? The one that is yours or the one that is not yours? What does your *inner knowing* tell you about this?

What if all you had to do was *choose* to *release it* and then *acknowledge and communicate with your body* every day, take whatever action was appropriate in that *now moment,* and allow your body to bring itself back into *its own natural balance?*

I can attest to the fact that as soon as you become aware that your condition is really *not* yours, that it instantly makes it easier to release! This was my direct experience. When I was very little, I had the *direct inner knowing* that *my* body was meant to live a very long, healthy life in a state of constant rejuvenation. This was very confusing to me, since I saw no evidence of this happening for anyone else. Everyone eventually 'grew old' and became frail. Because the 'evidence' in the world around me seemed to directly contradict my inner knowing, I thought that I had to *give up my knowing* to conform to the world around me.

Growing up with a strong, healthy athlete body, I never gave my health much thought. However, I began to 'buy into' the 'programming' that said *you'll get out of shape, you'll get fat, you're prone to diseases,* and such. Guess what began to happen?

As these things began to manifest, I fell out of trust with my body and began to resent it for 'falling out' of it's natural health and fitness. I felt that my body was betraying me. However, it was *I* who had inadvertently ‹betrayed› my body...I had given up my inner knowing.

Finally one day, when my body was the most out of balance, I had a sudden flash of insight. I suddenly remembered that *original inner knowing*...the original Truth that I was born with: that *my* body was meant to be strong, fit and healthy for a very long time. In a flash, it became perfectly clear to me: the physical imbalances were *NOT* 'mine'...I had picked up on the mass-consciousness programming! The imbalances had come from the hologram around me, they didn't originate from within me. In that moment it all became completely obvious to me. As soon as that became clear, it became infinitely faster and easier for my body to rebalance itself.

As soon as I chose that none of the imbalances were mine, (as I 'hopped in the car to drive' to from *imbalance* to *health*) I immediately began to feel more comfortable in my body. Soon, many other 'pieces of the puzzle' started to fall into place. The level of communication between me and my body became greatly enhanced. I was able to start trusting my body again because I realized it was not my body's 'fault', but rather the belief systems I had picked up from other people...I was *inadvertently* ‹embodying› other people›s reailty! *Oops!*

Would you allow yourself to *know* that your imbalance is NOT yours? Will you allow yourself to *choose* that?

Where did it come from? The choice is up to you.

Would you allow yourself to say, *"Oops!"* and return yourself to *Your* reality?

Tool 4. Feel

Manifestation happens is through vibrational alignment.

What does that mean?

Okay...remember when we talked about how everything starts out in the non-physical realms before it is made physical?

Well...here's how this works. When a choice is made to bring something into the physical realms, it is chosen from the non-physical realms where all possibilities exist. This means that your choice *already exists* as potential in the non-physical realms. If it didn't *already exist*...if it was not a viable possibility...you wouldn't be able to imagine it. Have you ever heard the expression *if you can dream it, you can do it?* It's true!

In order for something to be 'moved' from the non-physical to the physical, we must bring the physical realm (ourselves) into *vibrational harmony* with the item in the non-physical realms.

Okaaaay...sooo...how do we do that?

Well...we have to match our vibration with the vibration of the thing we are seeking to make manifest.

Do tell....

Okay! Here's the scoop! If you want to experience vibrant, radiant health...then you have to match yourself to that. You have to **choose** vibrant, radiant health...then you have to **feel** it on a *consistent basis* and you have to **know** that it is in the process of being made manifest. As an Infinite Being, you already ARE all things...radiant health is already contained inside you! In order to experience something in the physical, all you have to do is project that out into the world from within yourself.

If you desire to experience love, then project love. If you wish to experience health, then project well-being out into the world.

You have to consistently bring yourself into the *feeling* of what you are choosing. This will involve taking a few minutes, a few times each day, and *imagining* what vibrant, radiant health feels like. You'll know that you're *really* in the feel of it when the smile appears on your face and you start to feel light and expansive. Do this as often as you can.

What you're doing is *re-training* yourself into a new state of being. You've been in the *habit* of 'un-health' or 'imbalance', so now you'll need to *re-set* that to 'vibrant, radiant health'...and you do this through *feeling* and *knowing*.

Why do you keep using those words **vibrant** *and* **radiant?**

Good question!

Can you *feel* the expansiveness of those words? If you're just focused on *health* by itself, that's fine. But can you feel how 'flat' that word is? When we add the words *vibrant* and *radiant* to health, can you *feel* the difference?

Can you feel the *vitality, optimism* and *life* in the word *vibrant?*

Can you feel how *radiant* just *beams* and *shines* outward *and inward* in all directions?

Can you feel the difference between choosing *health* and choosing *vibrant, radiant health?* The words *vibrant* and *radiant* serve to enhance, expand and empower your choice for health. Feel free to choose your own words to enhance and empower your choice for health!

Use words that *feel good* to you! Use words that inspire you, that you can feel passionate about and that bring a smile to both your heart and your face! The more joy, passion and inspiration you can feel on a daily basis through visualizing and feeling into your new choice, the faster you'll bring yourself into resonance with it and the faster it will show up in your reality.

When you're switching your set-point from a *negative* one to a *positive* one...*GO BIG! Overshoot the mark!* Instead of just getting 'healthy'...*go for the body of your dreams! Hell...go for the LIFE of your dreams!*

Remember: You Are a *grand, infinite CREATOR!* You can create *anything* you desire!

The Creator's DNA runs through your DNA. Not only are you *like* God, *You* and *God* are made of the *same substance!* The Creator made you *in it's own image*...giving you *full creator abilities!* You've just been playing here on Earth with the veil over your head which caused you forget that little detail!

So...here's your opportunity to *choose* whatever it is that you would like to experience... and *feel* your way into alignment with it!

What will you choose?

Tool 5. Release the Limiting Beliefs and Thought Patterns

Here's a simple way to release any limiting beliefs or thought patterns that may appear:

Become aware of the You that feels limited (this is easy...it feels bad), and also become aware of the YOU that is ready to release it...the Infinite, Unlimited You that knows that something more expansive and joyful is also available. You'll notice that there is a difference! This is KEY! Take a few moments until you can see both aspects...the You that feels small and limited...and the Infinite You that realizes that there is a different option available.

Notice how the Infinite YOU that is ready to release the limitation is 'infinitely' more expansive and free than the 'limited You' that feels bad.

Are you now aware of both aspects? Great! Because from this perspective, when you can see that there is more to you than the aspect that is experiencing the limitation, you can realize that releasing the limitation is simply a matter of changing perspectives from the 'limited you' to the Expanded You.

To release the limiting belief, stand firmly in the Expanded You...the part of you that is infinite...the part that knows something grander is available. Take a few moment to really FEEL into the Infinite You...feel the lightness, ease, freedom and expansion you desire...that your Soul *already IS*. Feel into the beautiful Being You Are on the inside...breathe into the core of You. Breathe for a few seconds or a few minutes until you are breathing as the Infinite, Unlimited Being You Are.

Now...WITHOUT MOVING from this expansive space... without 'going to'...simply observe the limitation you were feeling. Look at how small it seems from this expanded space of the Infinite You. As you observe the limitation from this expansive space, allow it to dissolve. It was just a limited perspective...a distortion in the flow of unlimited energies. Let it go. Allow it to be released. Allow the Universe to flow through the distortion and re-harmonize it.

The key to this exercise is to be able to notice, when you are feeling limited, that there is an unlimited part of you, as well. By becoming adept at being aware of both parts simultaneously, you will begin to easily release the limitations that no longer serve You.

Tool 6. Ask the Angels

Now that you've chosen to dive into the world of Self Healing, that doesn't mean that you have to do it all by yourself. There are angels all around you who are just waiting to contribute to you in any way they can.

Remember...you've been playing this game underneath the veil of forgetfulness. The veil not only caused you to forget who You are, it also caused you to forget about the legions of angels... your friends...who stayed in the non-physical realms. They are here with you right now...they have never left your side.

The angels are very real, regardless of whether we can see them or not. In fact, WE are angels! We are angels who have chosen to play in the physical realms. The angels who have stayed in the non-physical realms have been at our sides, loving us, the whole time we've been living under our veils. They know that we are playing the game...they know that we've temporarily forgotten about them...and they are still right next to us cheering us on...no matter what we do. The angels know that there is absolutely nothing wrong with us! They have great love, honor and admiration for us to be so brave as to come here and forget who we are. Therefore, they never judge us...they only love and support us.

The angels can't heal us, since that is *our own* job...but they *can* assist us! And they are ready, willing and able to answer the call! *All we have to do is ask!*

If you're still a little skeptical about angels...ask for a sign. Ask the angles to send you a sign that they are with you...a sign that you can't possibly overlook or misinterpret...then pay attention as you move through your day. You can even ask for a specific sign, such as a feather or a butterfly.

Connecting to the angels is easy and fun! It's really just a matter of expanding your point of perception. The angels communicate through the heart, rather than through the mind. It's important to quiet the mind and open up to that place within yourself where the still, small voice of your Inner Being resides.

One of my favorite ways to receive information from the angelic realm is to ask a question then write down whatever comes to mind. Don't think...just write. You'll probably feel that *'it's just you'* writing, so at first you might be inclined to dismiss the information, but be persistent. You are intimately connected to the angelic realm...you ARE an angel...you just happen to be currently playing here in this physical game! Remember the analogy of the ocean? You and the angels are all particles of the grand ocean of the All That Is. The information from the angelic realms is transmitted through your Higher Self, which feels surprisingly just like...YOU! So don't dismiss the answers you receive and write down simply because you think that *this is silly...it's just me!* Would you be willing to *trust* YOU? Would you be willing to trust that you're receiving expanded wisdom from the angelic realms?

Once you begin asking for assistance from the Angels, be sure to open up your awareness to signs all around you. The Angels will communicate with you through all kinds of different symbols: through songs, books, cloud shapes, birds, animals, bumper stickers, billboards, paintings...the list is endless.

How does this work?

Well, let's look at a few examples. Let's say that you've sat quietly and asked for guidance about your body. You get up and go to your computer and find an email newsletter that has an article about the benefits of asparagus. Later in the morning you turn on the TV and you see someone cooking asparagus. Later in the day you go to the grocery store and asparagus is on sale. Might the angels be guiding you to add some asparagus to your diet?

Perhaps you've asked for confirmation that you're connecting to the angels and when you get into your car, you turn on the radio and *Angel* by Sarah McLachlan is playing. You get out of your car, glance up at the sky and notice a cloud that is shaped like an angel. You walk down the street and notice a painting of an angel hanging in a shop window. These are the confirmations you've been asking for...will you notice them?

You've been going through a difficult time and you ask the angels for a message. Suddenly you begin to notice deer: a deer in a field, a photo of a deer, a deer statue, the John Deere tractor symbol. As you notice this recurring image, you decide to look up the Native American medicine symbol for Deer and you find that it symbolizes gentleness. You then realize that you have been very hard on yourself lately. The angels are asking you to be kind to yourself and give yourself some gentle love and nurturing.

There are infinite ways in which the angels can send you messages. It is your job to be alert and aware in order to receive them. When you ask, they answer. Always. If you're not perceiving the answer, be sure to open your awareness. Are you too busy searching for signs instead of allowing them to come to you? Are you missing the subtler signs? Did you miss the wave of love they sent you? Did you notice the happy little butterfly that landed on the flower next to you?

When you first start communicating with the angels, be sure to ask that their messages be clear...things that you can't possibly overlook. They will send you all kinds of messages until you start noticing them. Once you start to notice, the Angels will then know which types of messages to send you. As you get more proficient with receiving the messages, you'll develop clear and easy communication.

You have a huge team of angelic assistants and they are thrilled to help you! Ask for guidance and inspiration! Just keep in mind that they are not there to heal you, fix you (you are not broken!), or *do it for you*. They are always with you and they offer their unending love, support and guidance. All you have to do is ask.

If you're just beginning to learn to connect to the angels, **oracle cards** are a very fun and interesting way to learn to connect to the angels. There are many specialized decks of oracle cards dedicated to the angels and their wisdom. The way this works is through your intention. You sit quietly, ask the angels for guidance and insight, then ask a question and draw a card. Look at the card and see what message comes to mind. Then you can refer to the booklet that comes with the cards that explains the meaning of that card. You'll be amazed at the level of clarity you'll receive! This is a great way for you to begin receiving clear messages from the angels. By having a physical card and written interpretation, it makes the messages clear and easy to understand. As you become comfortable using the cards, you'll soon become comfortable communicating in other ways as well.

Tool 7. Using Drawing and Sound as Tools to Harmonize

My friend **Rosemary Marchetta** has created this section of the book especially for us! She has combined her knowledge of the healing powers of both *sound* and *art* to create this special section that is designed as a tool to bring body, mind and spirit into harmony.

We are impacted and influenced by sound in multitudinous ways. In addition to the audible sounds our bodies can produce, our bodies are also emitting inaudible sound frequencies. When our frequencies are disharmonious, our bodies reflect that discord on a cellular level. If we harmonize our cellular frequencies, we can bring our bodies back into health and balance.

Harmonic Doodling (**harmonicdoodling.blogspot.com**) is a wonderful way to 'see' the inaudible song your body is singing. By seeing your song, you can then begin to consciously change it.

Being of Sound Mind and Body
by Rosemary Marchetta

Introduction

The word *sound* brings to mind all things auditory, as in what happens when a tree falls in the woods. Additionally, the word *sound*, as an adjective, can be defined as *'healthy, in good condition,'* *synonymous* with fit, flawless, vigorous or whole. Disease, on the other hand, can be described as a disorder, a deviation from the normal structure, a state of imbalance or being in *un*sound condition. Many ancient cultures, including Australian Aborigines, Egyptians and Greeks used the vibrational properties of sound to heal, in other words, they used sound to bring matter into a sound condition, but the practice was generally lost in the west until the fairly recent discovery of medicinal uses for ultrasound. Contemporary sound healing generally focuses on the principles of resonance and raising the vibrational frequency through conscious intention to promote health. The practices described here are simple techniques to bring our conscious awareness to focus on the vibrational frequencies of sound, allowing us to enter a relaxed, meditative state.

Using a pencil as a conscious tool we bring our focused attention to the structure and form of sound by drawing the shape of a particular tone. Drawing harmonic shapes helps us to enter into a meditative state and access the feeling of well being. Drawing specific areas of discomfort or dissonance helps us become more quiet, focused, and in tune with our inner workings. Drawing the shapes of sound can be thought of as steps to becoming aware of the vibrational frequencies that course though our physical, mental, and emotional bodies, and, by entering into harmonious resonance with certain tones, we can consciously alter these frequencies to become uplifted and enjoy a state of tranquil well-being.

A *doodle* is a drawing made while a person's attention is occupied by something other than the act of drawing. In the examples below we focus our attention on a particular sound tone or mantra, and use the pencil to create a representation of that tone on a page. There is no right or wrong doodle, only continuous flowing lines and curves that move into each other in an organic pattern. Harmonious tones are pleasing to the ear, and the resulting doodles are playful shapes that ease the mind. It is interesting to keep a doodle journal in which you freely fill the pages with shapes of the sounds you focus on. I recommend writing down the date and other relevant information alongside the doodle, whether it is a mantra, tone, or doodle of physical or emotional dissonance, etc. It is fun to look back on these doodles and read them like a journal entry, a description of the state of your life.

Harmonic Doodling: An approach to instantly creating a state of ease and harmony using a pencil, paper and your own imagination.

Harmonic Doodling is the term that I use to describe the simple but empowering process of drawing rhythmic, organic shapes with your attention focused on a particular sound or tone. I prefer to listen to specific sound frequencies while doodling, many of which are available for free online, but this is not necessary. You can doodle while listening to all sorts of sound meditation music, nature sounds, Tibetan bowls, etc. You can doodle while chanting *om* either silently or out loud, or use any other mantra or tone. However, especially in the beginning, it is easier to focus when you are physically hearing one tone, such as solfeggio harmonic frequencies. Choose something that is pleasing to your ear, breathe deeply, quiet your mind, and let your pencil move.

As you begin to doodle, letting your pencil flow around the page, your mind relaxes and starts to wander freely. The doodle shapes reflect this unwinding. Keep the pencil moving, following the shape of the sound you are hearing. I tend to do short doodles and then connect them with flowing lines into larger masses. As your mind settles into the process, turn the page and start doodling on a fresh sheet of paper. You begin to notice that your mind is more focused, and the doodles are more delicate, more precise. Organic shapes emerge as one line flows into the next. You feel relaxed, happy. You are in a meditative state in which time stands still, and the world outside your doodle is irrelevant.

Harmonic doodling can be practiced at any time of day, but is especially useful to quiet the mind before bed. It is also helpful to sit down and doodle if you are feeling stressed or upset about something. It can instantly bring you into a relaxed state of mental clarity and emotional well being. Get up and go about the rest of your day maintaining this state of mind. Practice this technique a few times and get comfortable with it before moving on to the other types of doodles described below.

Step by Step Process for Harmonic Doodling

1. You will need at least 15 minutes. Sit in a quiet place with your doodle journal and a sharp pencil. Breathe deeply and relax.
2. Listen to or chant a particular tone.
3. On a blank sheet of paper begin to move your pencil around the shape of the sound, drawing its contours. Know that sound

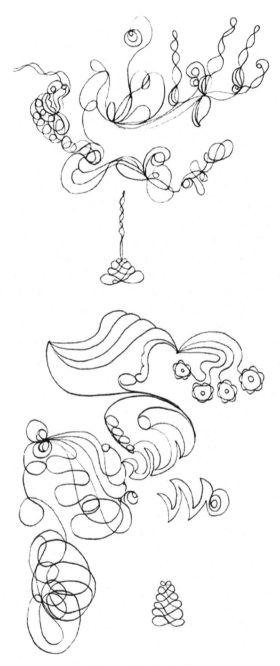

Harmonic Doodles

waves have form, and while placing your attention on this, allow the pencil to move freely around the page.

4. Stop and begin anew whenever you feel like it. Connect one doodle to another with flowing lines, enjoying the process.

5. After a few minutes you find that your mind has relaxed and there is less resistance to the drawing.

6. Start on a new page and continue doodling in the same relaxed manner. You will now see that your mind is more relaxed and alert, and your doodles are more refined.

7. When you finish doodling, notice this peaceful state of mind, and reflect on this as you go about your day.

Doodle to Diffuse, Balance, and Harmonize

Now that you are familiar with harmonic doodling you might want to go further, using the practice of doodling to alter the energy patterns you perceive. Find an area in your body where you are experiencing discomfort. Alternatively, it could be a mental or an emotional space where the energy feels stuck. Breathe deeply and quiet your mind. Draw a rectangle on your page that symbolically marks the boundaries of the problem area. In the center of the rectangle draw a shape that represents the area of discomfort. This can be an abstract shape or a simple rectangle or circle that you use to represent the area you want to alter. Keeping your attention focused on that area of your body or mind, use your pencil to bring lines from this center shape out towards the border rectangle. If it feels right, have the lines cross the border and go out to the space around the rectangle. Trust your intuition. The lines may be ripple patterns, or branching lines that reach out to the border. The shape of the lines do not matter as much as the conscious awareness of the action of the pencil. Be intentional, feeling the intensity of the central area diminish as you radiate outwards with your pencil.

Continue drawing as you breathe deeply. If necessary, draw a second rectangle after the first one is complete. As your starting point, use the already diminished area of tension from the previous drawing, continuing to release as the pencil lines spread outward.

When you have completed this process you could create a harmonic doodle for this area, mentally superimposing this harmonic image and sound tone over the original area of discomfort. Breathe deeply and notice a feeling of release, akin to opening a window to let fresh air into a stuffy room. Use this technique to quickly defuse anger, worry or other negative thought patterns that you want to release.

Step by Step Process for Doodling to Diffuse

1. You will need at least 15 minutes. Sit in a quiet place with your doodle journal and a sharp pencil. Breathe deeply and relax.
2. Determine a particular area of discomfort in your mind or body and draw a rectangle on the page that symbolizes the borders of this problem.
3. Draw a shape in the center of the rectangle that symbolizes the area of discomfort.
4. Slowly and intentionally use your pencil to draw out the negative, stuck feeling, bringing the pencil lines from the center towards the border. Fill the rectangle with these lines. Continue to breathe deeply.
5. Repeat the process with a new rectangle to further diminish the intensity.

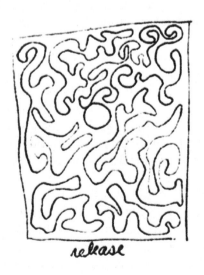

release

defuse

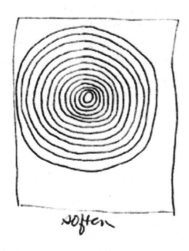

softer

harmonize

6. Create a harmonic doodle with a sound tone and mentally superimpose this tone and image over the original area of discomfort to harmonize and balance the energies there.

Inner-focus Drawing

Inner-focus drawing is a method for gaining insight into the specifics of a physical, mental, or emotional problem area. The idea is to focus your attention on an area where you feel discomfort, and then use your in-sight to make marks on a page that resemble the situation. It is different from the other types of doodling which are a series of repetitive or flowing lines. These are graphic representations of your pain, frustration, or sadness. The marks are expressive. They may be bold or delicate, but they are made with precise awareness.

To begin, draw a rectangular border encompassing most of the page, while leaving some space around the edges in case you feel it is necessary to make some marks outside the border. Focus your attention on the area of discomfort. Breathe deeply. If it is a physical part of your body you may want to place your other hand over the area and close your eyes while you envision what that area looks like before proceeding. If it is a mental or emotional problem, place your awareness on the area of discomfort in order to 'see' it clearly. Begin to make marks on the page using the pencil expressively, not really being concerned with what the drawing looks like. Scribble in or outline over areas that feel like they need it. You can use an eraser if you feel some of the marks aren't quite right. Use your intuition, and keep breathing. Continue until you feel that the pencil marks are an adequate representation of your problem area. The process is similar to constructing a well-formed written paragraph, but you are using expressive marks, rather than an alphabet, to make your statement.

When you have finished, study your drawing. Ask yourself what the lines mean, and gather what insight you can from the image. Often, there is a lot of information about our feelings and thoughts that lie just under our conscious awareness. Through the act of drawing we can bring this information to the surface and into our consciousness. Then we can make a well-informed decision about the best way to proceed forward towards resolution of the problem. I find it convenient to write down the title of the drawing, for example 'My Spleen' or 'My Relationship with X', along with any insights or ideas gathered from the process, on the back of the page or right next to the drawing. Don't judge yourself, or censor the information, just write it down. Go back and read these notes later, and add anything else that is relevant. Sometimes more insights bubble up to our consciousness as time passes. If it feels right, at this point you can create a doodle for this specific area with the intention of defusing or releasing the tension held there.

Step by Step Process for Inner-focus Drawing

1. You will need about 15 minutes. Sit in a quiet place with your doodle journal and a sharp pencil. Breathe deeply and relax.
2. Draw a large rectangle using most of the page, leaving some space for the drawing to spill over outside the border.
3. Focusing your awareness on the area of discomfort make expressive marks that represent this area. Compose carefully, continuing to breathe, and using your intuition to make pencil marks that create an accurate representation of the problem.
4. When you have finished, 'read' the drawing to gain insight into the situation. Write this information next to the drawing.

Inner focus drawing of My Spleen

5. Go back and revisit the drawing later, adding any fresh insights that occur to you.
6. Harmonize the area with a tone and harmonic doodle.

Conclusion

These methods for creating doodles are designed as a tool for self empowerment. By becoming more aware of harmony, we also become more aware of any dissonance that might exist in our space. We can choose to eliminate the dissonance by being in resonance with harmony, and we can create that state of harmony through doodling. This is most easily understood through the act of doodling, and then experiencing that peaceful state of ease. It is a state of well being in which everything feels right with the world and healing can occur.

It is best to begin your practice with harmonic doodling, filling several pages in different sessions before moving on to the other methods. The more frequently you doodle, the easier it becomes to align your energies with the harmonic tones you are hearing.

Developing Finished Doodles

Although the main reason for doodling is to become aware of and align with harmonic sounds, it is very satisfying to see the beautiful imagery emerge on the pages of your journal. If you want to develop these doodles into more complete drawings you can trace them, or parts of them, onto a fresh sheet of paper, rotating and flipping the doodle to create symmetry and kaleidoscope effects. Add straight lines, color them in, or add details to create a finished piece.

Happy Doodling! —Rosemary

Section Six:
Stories of Self Healing

This section contains my own story of self-healing along with my friend Kathy Bradley's story. We both want you to know that self-healing is most definitely possible by following your inner guidance.

Kathy's Story

Kathy Bradley (**www.KathyBradleyandtheAngels.com**) is a Reiki Master and spiritual counselor. She was inspired to share her story of self-healing with you. She regularly works with the angels and offers personalized guidance from the angelic realms for her clients.

> *"The journey of a thousand miles, begins with one step"*
> —*Lao Tzu*

My spiritual journey began in 1995. I had undergone back surgery, as I was in constant pain due to a ruptured disc, L5S1, to be exact. After going through the rehabilitation and still finding myself in pain, I was looking at yet another surgery. I decided to look for other holistic options. Here I was in all this pain, and conventional medicine was not the answer for me. I had to dig deeper. I needed to look below the surface of the "ruptured disc." This is when my search began.

This is when I found Reiki. I had learned through my studies with Reiki that dis-ease in the body typically begins in the mental and emotional bodies. The pain then manifests in the physical body. I soon realized that my pain stemmed from a combination of fear, guilt and self-judgment. I deemed myself to be unworthy of love; unworthy of self-respect. I was well programmed. What I mean by being programed, is that we are all brought up with outside sources, such as our Mother/Father, priest or teacher who we allow to dictate our personal worth. I just think back to the teacher who said I'm an embarrassment to my family, or the prayer that states I am not worthy. We've all had these things happen to us. Little by little, we start believing "I'm not good enough." And so it was, I was believing I'm not a good mother, wife, daughter, sister, and on and on. You fill in the blank!

All of the negative thoughts and feelings create dis-ease in the body.

The first step back to health is becoming aware that this is occurring and to acknowledge it. The second step is deciding what to do about it. Will you continue down this path of self misery or will you chose to see yourself as worthy? Will you look at yourself with compassion and forgiveness and choose to deserve something better? I remember meeting a Zen master and we were talking about being angry with ourselves. He told me of the tree...and how the tree would not be so foolish to fight among its branches! This made a lot of sense to me. After this I made a decision to work on loving all of the parts of myself, even the shadow side.

During this time, I became tuned into the energy; the energy of my spirit, the energy of my emotions, the energy of my physical body. Once I decided enough already...I understood the connection, and was aware of the healing that was taking place. It was truly miraculous: the constant pain had subsided while I was taking a Reiki class! The crazy thing is that I questioned it! How could the pain be gone? I was filled with disbelief. Could I have healed myself? As I was questioning this healing, I put the TV on as I was getting ready to go back to complete my Reiki course. On the TV was an evangelical who was quoting Jesus, and was saying "I say unto you, he that believeth in me the works that I do, shall he do also, and greater works than these." I just had to believe in myself! This was a confirmation that it was possible, and that it did in fact happen.

This brought me to a place to begin looking within myself, not outside of myself for the answers. Look within, not outside yourself...within your hearts and realize that the only judge in sight is yourself. Even if there was something that you felt you needed to judge yourself for...drop it. Let it go. Your creator has long since forgiven you. Won't you do the same?

The pivotal point was to change my life by choosing new thoughts, words and deeds. Everything has its own frequency, or vibration, including thoughts and emotions. Energy attracts similar energy. Like attracts like.

Did you ever notice that people keep attracting the same experiences over and over? Some are always lucky, and some aren't. Some attract dysfunctional relationships while others attract happy relationships. No matter how hard they "try" people will keep attracting the same circumstances again and again.

You attract what you vibrate to. Like attracts like. Right now in this present moment of now, you can chose to use positive words and affirmations. Let go of the judgments, and know you are doing the best you can. We can look at our lives and know that everything happens exactly as it's supposed to and that some of the darkest moments bring the greatest epiphanies or opportunities. Now look out to the future and see how much brighter it appears. You see, all of the past taught us many, many lessons. Let go of the fear and worry, and allow the love and light to fill your hearts.

We are responsible for our own lives. We are the only ones that can decide to put ourselves first. At the end of the day it doesn't matter if you've "helped" everyone else, if you first have not taken care of yourself. Your first priority is yourself. It is ok to be "selfish." I was raised to put other's needs ahead of my own. This is not the way. We need to put ourselves first. You can't offer someone a cup of water if the well is dry, can you? Take the time each day to pray, mediate, go out in nature, play with oracle cards or tools of divination. They are most helpful in offering you guidance.

As you tend the alter of life, you are surrounded by spiritual support and protection. It is within the air you breath, the sky above, and the earth below. Personally symbolic objects come into your life as visible, tangible signs of the grace and power that are your natural birthright. Regard these sacred objects and your sanctified space with respect and reverence. Let your sacred objects become part of your ritual of prayers. Allow your reverence for these holy objects to teach you to revere all life, and have faith that it will help you balance the spiritual and physical in yourself. All of the elements are there to offer us guidance. Whether it be the Angelic realm, the plant realm or the crystal realm. They are available to offer us support. We just need to be open to receiving the gifts and messages as they come to us and to believe they are real. The format may include looking at a beautiful piece of art, or in nature listening to a babbling brook, or while driving your car listening to your favorite music. It matters not, as long as it raises your vibrations and attunes you to your Divinity.

Traveling to Sedona, I bought a deck of Doreen Virtue's oracle cards. Immediately I was able to receive daily Angelic guidance of love and light. The positive messages and guidance were so helpful in creating a sense of peace in my life that I later studied with Doreen Virtue in Hawaii.

We have so many tools out there that can assist us on our journey back to health and well-being. We have all of the tools we need to change our lives. If we believe anything is possible, it is. Truly anything! The possibilities are endless. Take the time to connect with your higher self, and say from your heart "I am an enlightened being." What is it that I want to create in my life. When you do this exercise, do it with a smile in your heart, and be happy with yourself. It doesn't have to be heavy or serious. Rather, make it fun.

The energies of joy are high vibrational, and will take you out of your mind and into your heart. This is where you will find the answers, from within your heart. It is simple. The energies that are pouring in are of high vibrational energy. Chose to align yourself with vibrant health and prosperity. With joy. With peace. With love. You are a sovereign being. Take back your power. Say "I Am that I Am" and allow all of these joyous energies to come flowing to you. Live the life you were born to live.

Love, Kathy

My Story

The moment I realized I was facing cancer I froze in terror. I had been denying the telltale signals my body had been sending me. I was angry with my body for giving me such trouble. Why wasn't it just being healthy? Why was my body in such disharmony? I had been on 'the spiritual path' for a long time. I knew that I was creating my own reality…so why was this physical distress showing up? Shouldn't I be getting healthier as my consciousness was expanding?

What I didn't realize at the time was that *resentment* was a very strong emotion that was very actively running in the background of my subconscious mind. The physical symptoms emanating from my body were the signals telling me that I had some misaligned beliefs that were causing disharmony in my reality. Even though I instinctively knew this, I was still resentful of my body and my reality. However, because I was fully aware that somehow *I* was the one creating this 'mess' for myself, I knew that it was time for me to uncover the patterns that were sabotaging my health and my happiness.

I knew that *I* was the one who would ultimately have to heal myself, with or without conventional medicine. I knew that modern medicine and pharmaceuticals were not right for me. I intuitively knew that I needed to take a different approach. I knew that if I was going to become truly masterful in this lifetime, that I would have to work this out for myself, working from the inside out.

I understood the concept that my thoughts were creating my reality, and I knew that I was harboring many disempowering beliefs. But this was the turning point: this was the point where *the rubber meets the road*. I needed to *embody my knowing*. It was no longer an option to keep my *knowing* in my cognitive mind; I had to bring that knowing into my heart and I had to start *living my knowing*.

My decision to go it alone was not an easy one. My cognitive mind, in it's attempt to keep me 'safe,' kept screaming at me that I was crazy to try to change my body by changing my mind. Now, in retrospect, I can see how my mind was really trying to protect *itself!* However, through it all, the still, small voice within my Heart was telling me that there *was* another way and that it was important that I discover how to heal myself. I knew that I had to trust my Heart. I knew that I was taking full responsibility for my own health. I knew that my choice was unconventional and that if it backfired on me and I wasn't able to bring my body back into balance, that no one would be able to understand.

My path back to balanced health wasn't particularly smooth or graceful, I must admit! I spent many dark nights being angry, depressed and resentful of my body. But through it all, I kept listening to the deep inner voice that said that all would be okay. So I kept doing the spiritual work. I knew that I was harboring disempowering beliefs that had caused the condition to manifest in the first place, so I kept digging and uncovering the beliefs that were holding me back. I learned to breathe and release. I strengthened my muscle testing skills so that I could start communicating more clearly with my body. I learned to ground and clear my energy. I learned to ask for assistance from the angelic realms. I learned how to release my limiting belief patterns.

During the process, I came to find out that I was not really in my body! I had no idea that it was even possible to *not* be in our bodies, but I came to learn that most humans are not fully present in their bodies.

I began to study with Jim Self in his Mastering Alchemy program, where I learned more about keeping my electromagnetic field clear and balanced. I learned techniques that allowed me to begin pulling more of my soul essence back inside my body. As I began to merge my essence back into my body, the insights became more frequent and more clear. I began to recognize the patterns of powerlessness and resentment I was running. As my soul began to merge more fully with my body, I began to see my body through my soul's eyes...I began to know the natural well-being that I Am. I began to focus on the vibrant, radiant health that is natural to my Inner Being.

Then, one day, the pattern became clear that I was being both the victim and the perpetrator...of a 'condition' that wasn't actually a 'condition' after all! The vision was so clear that it made me laugh out loud that that scenario was even possible! When I got through laughing, I cleared the pattern by making the clear choice to stop it. I gathered up all of the energy...felt it fully...then breathed it out and released it. That was the moment my body began to rebalance itself. I continued to focus on the vibrant, radiant health that I *knew was mine*, and watched as my body responded accordingly.

Today, I am actually grateful for my experience! I am grateful because I realized that 'disease' is not at all what we've been taught to believe it is. I learned that it isn't even as *real* as we've been taught! Through my experience, I have now seen through the entire illusion of *disease*. I have absolutely no more fear of cancer, or any other disease, because I know the truth about them. I recognized them for the illusions that they are, and learned that once you look an illusion squarely in the face...it dissolves. It was just an illusion that I had thought was real.

I will never experience disease in my own reality again. Why? Because once you know the full *Truth* about an illusion that you once thought was real, you see that it was all smoke and mirrors and you take all of your power back from it. The entire issue is resolved energetically and it simply dissolves forever from your reality. It is no longer an item on the 'buffet table.'

Are *You* willing to allow all disease to dissolve from *Your* reality?

My path of self-healing was very unconventional according to current standards and I definitely don't recommend it. Frankly, I don't *recommend* anything...other than *following your own inner knowing!* Self-Healing takes a lot of courage, a lot of self-trust, and a willingness to take *full responsibility* for your own health...no matter what. If you are still here reading...give yourself a HUGE pat on the back...because You, my friend, are one of the ones who is willing! You are a Self-Empowered human angel! You are willing to take full responsibility for yourself and your creations! That is HUGE! *Congratulations!*

Not all humans are ready for this level of responisbility. Not all humans are ready to take full responsibility for their own bodies, their own health, their own happiness and certainly not for their own *lives!* You, my dear reader, are different. You *are* willing. You are one who is changing the world. You are one who is bringing health, harmony, balance and LOVE back to the planet! THANK YOU!

There are many paths to radiant health...as many paths as there are people. If you are currently rebalancing your body, know that you cannot choose the 'wrong' path. Whichever path you choose, is YOUR choice. Trust your choices. No other Being in the entire Universe knows you better than YOU...listen to the whispers of *your* Soul. Know what *You* know. Trust Your Knowing.

And remember: your body loves you! It is not your enemy. There is no need to try to run away from it or escape it. It is simply acting as a mirror, showing you how you perceive the world around you...showing you how you perceive...*You!*

You are a vibrant, radiant Being of Magnitude, my friend... wear it well. Allow your body to reflect *that!*

Many Blessings on your journey! —Lisa :-)

SECTION SEVEN:
Resources

I want to take this opportunity to acknowledge the people who have made a deep impression on my journey back to well-being. I am writing this book directly from my own knowledge, experience, and conscious awareness which have been greatly impacted and influenced by the teachings of these amazing Beings. Due to the profound impact these people's teachings have had on me, their teachings have become deeply, inextricably integrated into my Being and their energies and their teachings are directly influencing this book.

I'm choosing to include this section simply because these people and their offerings have been incredibly helpful to me and I know how profoundly grateful I was to have these resources to assist me on my journey back to health.

If you have resonated with the contents of this book, I wish to call your attention to these modern-day Masters, as the services they offer might be as beneficial to you as they have been for me. They are all amazing sources for comfort, inspiration, expansion and new awareness. If you feel drawn to any of them, here are the links for you to directly connect to them and explore the information and resources they have to offer:

The Crimson Circle (**CrimsonCircle.com**) messages of love and empowerment from Ascended Masters Tobias and Adamus St. Germain channeled through Geoffery Hoppe. The free monthly webcasts, which include news and updates about the happenings of the Crimson Circle along with the channeled messages (or 'shouds') have been a true godsend for me. They provide fun, thought-provoking humor, clear insight, deep love, and an entire 'family' of awakening humans (Shaumbra) who are all sharing the same journey into awakening. The Crimson Circle is a world-wide community of New Energy teachers, dedicated to expanding consciousness through messages and teachings of love, compassion and personal empowerment. Their website offers an extensive library of free materials, listings of upcoming classes and events around the globe, a free monthly webcast and a Forum for like-minded individuals to easily connect and offer support to one another. The Crimson Circle Store is filled with products, books, music, channeled messages, personal study materials, online courses and lots of 'freebies' thrown into the mix as well!

Mastering Alchemy (**MasteringAlchemy.com**) tools for navigating these shifting times within ourselves and on our planet. A pathway to ascension designed by the Archangels and Ascended Masters taught through Jim Self. The Mastering Alchemy website as well as Jim's YouTube page offer a wealth of free practical tools and information in addition to the core Mastering Alchemy classes. Jim explains what is taking place within humanity and upon our planet during this massive shift of consciousness we are experiencing, and he offers simple, practical tools and techniques for managing our energetic fields and releasing old patterns that no longer serve us. His Conversations With Jim Self is a monthly radio program that Jim hosts on Awakening Zone Radio (**AwakeningZone.com**). It is a series of enlightening and informative conversations with some of the most interesting and well-informed teachers, channels and authors in the world today. Jim and Roxane Burnett have written an extremely informative book: *What do You Mean the Third Dimension is Going Away?–Why now is the time to release who you are not and remember who you are.* I highly recommend this book for a clear, concise overview of the shift of consciousness that is occurring upon our planet and within ourselves. It is chock-full of practical information and powerful tools and practices to help us navigate smoothly through these rapidly changing times.

Rikka Zimmerman (**RikkaZimmerman.com**) is a facilitator of expanding consciousness through her programs of Adventures in Oneness. Rikka has an amazing capacity to set people free from the illusions of this reality through instantaneous shifts of awareness. Rikka is a beautiful, bright light and a true Master of human consciousness. She has the incredible ability to see through any illusion that Third Dimensional reality has to offer. As she stands firmly rooted in the higher dimensions, she has the gift of being able to spontaneously shatter illusions and guide people into higher dimensional awareness. Here are the links where you can listen to some of her free offerings or check out the archive of a free live stream event. She is one of the most highly sought-after guest speakers for webinar series such as You Wealth Revolution, Messenger Revolution and Healing with the Masters. It was on these series of interviews that I became aware of Rikka, Dr. Dain Heer and other amazing speakers like Panache Desai. I highly recommend these types of free webinars to help expand your realm of awareness. In addition to her skills as a facilitator of consciousness expansion, Rikka is also a singer, songwriter and recording artist! What if your consciousness could expand simply by listening to beautiful music?

The Messages of Kryon channeled through Lee Carroll (**Kryon. com**). The messages of Kryon were my introduction to my spiritual awakening. It was sometime in the mid-to late-90s when someone suggested I read The Journey Home. It was the very first channeled book I ever read, and the first time I discovered the concept that we create our own reality...I was hooked! It was the first time that something made absolute, total sense to me about the workings of this crazy reality in which we live. I wasn't sure at the time just where the message was coming from, but I knew that it was filled with Love with a capital 'L' and that the content was Truth with a capital 'T'. I then read every Kryon book I could get my hands on! On the website, there are hundreds of hours of free audio channels in the archives along with hundreds of archived transcripts dating back to 1997, which are still just as fresh and relevant today as they were in the moment they were first channeled.

Dr. Dain Heer (**DrDainHeer.com**) of Access Consciousness (**AccessConsciousness.com**) is the author of Being You, Changing the World. I first came across Dain when he was interviewed online by Jennifer McLean in her Healing with the Masters series. I had never heard of him before, but from the moment I began to listen, I immediately realized that he is the real deal. He is one of the most sincere and compassionate beings I've seen and I've gotten many amazing insights from his work. Access Consciousness is a very effective and useful method for eliminating limiting beliefs and opening up to new possibilities. Check out Dain's website or the Access Consciousness Store for a wide array of helpful books, audios and classes. Addditionally, the Access Bars® is a highly-effective, relaxing, in-person body process that helps neutralize the trapped energetic charges around all of the thoughts, beliefs, decisions, ideas and attitudes you've ever had about anything.

For deeply insightful guidance and inspiration, I highly recommend having a personalized Angel Reading from Kathy Bradley (**KathyBradleyandtheAngels.com**). I've had the honor of having her do readings for me, and it's amazing the depth of clarity, awareness and unconditional Love that comes through!

For further reading about how physical symptoms are linked to their energetic causes, Louise Hay's bestseller, You Can Heal Your Life is a classic!

At first glimpse, this reference might seem out of place, but I assure you it's not! Robert Scheinfeld's (**RobertScheinfeld.com**) book, Busting Loose from the Money Game was a huge inspiration for me! He explains in simple, scientific terms how the illusion of this reality is created. This book really helped me to see through the illusion and start taking my power back. Stepping out of the 'money game' is just the icing on the cake!

And last, but certainly not least, if you resonate with *this* book and would like some additional energetic support from *me*, visit my website at: **ConnectingYoutoYou.com**. As one who has already walked this path, I'm willing to help as many others as I can. I am currently offering private coaching sessions. Be sure to stay tuned for future books, classes and seminars!

There are many other wonderful authors, speakers and channelers who I greatly admire, but my list must stop somewhere. Those listed above have been at the core of my awakening. I hope you find one or more of them to be helpful to you, too!

About the Author

As a young child, Lisa was aware that there was much more to life than meets the eye. She knew that she was an Old Soul. She instinctively knew that the larger part of herself, her Soul, the part that is non-physical and never dies, was existing outside of this physical reality. She's spent much of this lifetime learning how to re-connect to  that Soul. When she realized that she had created disease in her body, she knew that it was time for that reconnection. She knew that she could reconnect by allowing her body to die, or she could reconnect while fully embodied. She chose the latter. Knowing that her Soul was always radiantly healthy, she set about releasing the distorted belief systems that were acting as a barrier between her body and her Soul. As the connection with her Soul grew stronger, so did her physical body. With every distorted belief she released, her body became healthier and her awareness expanded. As her awareness expanded, she began to see that everything that had been keeping her locked into various paradigms of dis-ease (from physical to financial) were simply distorted belief systems that were blocking the flow of her own well-Being. Today, she specializes in helping others release themselves from the paradigms of *dis*-ease. You can visit her website at: **ConnectingYoutoYou. com**.

Perfect For You
Perfect For Us

Unknown Identity Series
Unknown
Unexposed
Unsure
Unpublished

Standalone
Wash
Loving Charity
Summer Lovin'
Christmas Magic: A Romance Anthology
Love & College
Billionaire Heart
First Love
Frisky and Fun Romance Box Collection
Managing the Bosses Box Set #1-3

Manufactured by Amazon.ca
Bolton, ON